LARRY SANG'S

CHINESE ASTROLOGY & FENG SHUI GUIDE

2021

The Year of The Ox

with Lorraine Wilcox

LARRY SANG'S

The Year of The Ox
ASTROLOGY AND FENG SHUI GUIDE

Original Title:
Master Larry Sang's 2021 The Year of the Ox Astrology and Feng Shui Guide

Published by: The American Feng Shui Institute
7220 N. Rosemead Blvd., Suite 204
San Gabriel, CA 91775
Email: fsinfo@amfengshui.com
www.amfengshui.com

Written by:
Master Larry Sang

Edited by:
Lorraine Wilcox

Design, Illustration & Layout by:
Heidy Hon

Acknowledgment

This book would not be possible without the assistance of our brightest students and dear friends. Thank you Lorraine Wilcox for your wise input, editing, and translation. Thank you Heidy Hon for coordinating the layout, book cover, illustrations and keeping everything together, Chris Shaul for your expertise support and Zihan Zhang (張子涵) for your assistance with Sifu's calligraphy. Most of all, thank you to my wife Salina for your tireless love and support.

-Larry Sang

Please Read This Information

This book provides information regarding the subject matter covered. The authors are not engaged in rendering legal, medical or other professional advice. If you need medical or legal advice, a competent professional should be contacted. Chinese Astrology and Feng Shui are not get-rich-quick or cure-all schemes. Changes in your life will happen as fast as you are ready for them. Be patient in your study of Chinese Astrology and Feng Shui.

The authors have tried to make this book as complete and accurate as possible. However, there may be typographical or content mistakes. Use this book as a general guide in your study of Chinese Astrology and Feng Shui.

This book was written to educate and entertain. The authors, distributors and the American Feng Shui Institute shall have neither liability nor responsibility to any person with respect to any loss or damage caused, or alleged to be caused by this book.

The following pages of predictions will help you understand trends as they develop through the coming year. Please keep in mind that they are somewhat general because other stellar influences are operative, according to the month, date and exact minute of your birth. Unfortunately, we cannot deal with each person individually in this book.

Table of Contents

PART ONE: Chinese Astrology
Fortunes of the 12 Animals in the Year of The Ox

How to find your Animal Sign 6
The Ox 10
The Tiger 12
The Rabbit 14
The Dragon 16
The Snake 18
The Horse 20
The Sheep 22
The Monkey 24
The Rooster 26
The Dog 28
The Pig 30
The Rat 32
Li Ming for the Year 2021 35

PART TWO: Folk Methods of Fortune Telling

Liu Ren 41
Omens 47
The Yellow Emperor in the Four Seasons 51

PART THREE: Feng Shui Analysis and Remedies for 2021

Feng Shui 55
Preparing Your Home for a Reading 57
Directions to Avoid for Construction this Year 63
Feng Shui Energy (Qi) Pattern for 2021 64
The Center 66
The East Section 68
The Southeast Section 70
The South Section 72
The Southwest Section 74
The West Section 76
The Northwest Section 78
The North Section 80
The Northeast Section 82

PART FOUR: Day Selection Guide to the Year of The Ox

Day Selection 85
Calendar Terminology Key 87
12 Months of 2021 88
Ten-Thousand Year Calendar for 2021 115

How to find Your Animal Sign

In order to find your correct animal sign, as well as understand why the Chinese calendar begins in February, and not January, it is important to have a little understanding of the two different Chinese calendars. As with most things Chinese, we look at the Yin and Yang. In Chinese timekeeping, there is a Yin Calendar (Lunar calendar) and a Yang Calendar (Solar calendar).

The Lunar Calendar

The Lunar calendar is perhaps the best known and most popular of the two. Chinese Lunar New Year is frequently celebrated with a lot of pageantry. It is used in one type of Chinese Astrology called Zi Wei Dou Shu, and also in Yi Jing calculations.

The Solar Calendar

The Solar calendar is less well known. The early Chinese meteorologists attempts to gain insight into the cycles of the seasons. From this study, this developed the Solar calendar. This calendar is used in the form of Chinese Astrology called Four Pillars, as well as in Feng Shui. The Chinese were very accurate in their studies. Without computers, and using only observations, they mapped a solar year of 365 days. They missed the actual timing of a year by only 14 minutes and 12 seconds.

The solar year is divided into 24 solar terms. Each lasts about fifteen days. Spring Begins (lichun) is the name of the first day of Spring, and the first solar term. It is exactly midway between the winder solstice and the spring equinox. This is why it always falls on February 4th or 5th. We begin the five elements with Wood, so the Chinese New Year begins with a Wood month, whether in the Lunar or the Solar calendar. These concepts are derived from the Yi Jing.

*Aging can be moderated if
one takes a light view of
fame and wealth.
Virtual immortality can be
achieved if
one is free of wants
and worries.*

Calligraphy by Larry Sang

How to find your Animal Sign

To find your animal sign, Start with your birth date. If it is before February 4th (Spring Begins), use the prior year for the Chinese calendar. If it is after February 4th, then use the same birth year. If it is on February 4th, then you need the time of the birth to accurately determine the birth animal. This information is contained in the Chinese Ten-Thousand Year Calendar. (The American Feng Shui Institute has one available as an ebook at www.amfengshui.com). In the following pages, the birth years are listed for each animal, but remember, if your birthday is before February 4th, use the previous year to determine the animal.

The Twelve Animals

Rat 鼠	*Ox* 牛	*Tiger* 虎	*Rabbit* 兔
1924, 1936, 1948, 1960, 1972, 1984, 1996, 2008, 2020	1925, 1937, 1949, 1961, 1973, 1985, 1997, 2009, 2021	1926, 1938, 1950, 1962, 1974, 1986, 1998, 2010, 2022	1927, 1939, 1951, 1963, 1975, 1987, 1999, 2011, 2023
Dragon 龍	*Snake* 蛇	*Horse* 馬	*Sheep* 羊
1928, 1940, 1952, 1964, 1976, 1988, 2000, 2012, 2024	1929, 1941, 1953, 1965, 1977, 1989, 2001, 2013, 2025	1930, 1942, 1954, 1966, 1978, 1990, 2002, 2014, 2026	1931, 1943, 1955, 1967, 1979, 1991, 2003, 2015, 2027
Monkey 猴	*Rooster* 雞	*Dog* 狗	*Pig* 豬
1932, 1944, 1956, 1968, 1980, 1992, 2004, 2016, 2028	1933, 1945, 1957, 1969, 1981, 1993, 2005, 2017, 2029	1934, 1946, 1958, 1970, 1982, 1994, 2006, 2018, 2030	1935, 1947, 1959, 1971, 1983, 1995, 2007, 2019, 2031

FORTUNES OF THE 12 ANIMALS

The Ox

Note: The New Year begins February 3rd

After an auspicious year in 2020, it will be a challenging year for the Ox in 2021. Where career and jobs are concerned, the Ox will encounter a great deal of pressure and competition. With the Hua Gai star in Ming Palace, this will be a significant year in education for the Ox, with some important work projects and exams, as well as for choosing a subject to specialize in. The best time for you to proceed with your ambition is in the early spring and autumn. Money prospects are average. Income is slow and out-go is fast; therefore playing safe is the best policy. If you take an active stance, like going on overseas working trips or even vacation, avoid disputes with others while in foreign lands. Otherwise you may suffer financial losses or be hit by a lawsuit. Health-wise, there are no life-threatening illnesses. Those who were born in 1973 may encounter problems with the head. Beware of traffic accidents or injuries from sharp objects. Your love life is not as colorful as last year. Though you may date fairly often, it is difficult to differentiate a sincere relationship from one that is not, so it will be quite a while before you find true love. Married couples will be emotional, hot and cold, and easily aroused to argue and lose control.

Your Benefactor is: Dog
(1934, 1946, 1958, 1970, 1982, 1994, 2006, 2018)

12 Month Outlook For The Ox

Solar Month	Comments
1st Month Feb 3rd - Mar 4th	Luck is normal. Not too much excitement nor too many obstacles.
2nd Month Mar 5th - Apr 3rd	This is a relatively favorable month for relationships.
3rd Month Apr 4th - May 4th	Things are uncertain; knocks and bumps lie ahead. Avoid visiting the sick and attending funerals.
4th Month May 5th - Jun 4th	Be conservative. Don't be aggressive or make decisions in a hurry.
5th Month Jun 5th - Jul 6th	Good in money luck. Good for venturing overseas.
6th Month Jul 7th - Aug 6th	Money and peach blossom luck are strong. There is a sign of small consuming; budget wisely.
7th Month Aug 7th - Sep 6th	A big consuming star shines above; don't be greedy about money matters beyond your capability.
8th Month Sep 7th - Oct 7th	Auspicious stars shine above, good in all aspects.
9th Month Oct 8th - Nov 6th	Strong money luck. Good time to develop something new; things will be achieved in the right place and time.
10th Month Nov 7th - Dec 6th	Keep on high alert. Watch out for the flu or cuts.
11th Month Dec 7th - Jan 4th	Conditions stimulate you to try something different.
12th Month Jan 5th - Feb 3rd	Auspicious luck may bring you a benefactor during social activities.

The Tiger

1926, 1938, 1950, 1962, 1974, 1986, 1998, 2010

Note: The New Year begins February 3rd

The Ox year holds good fortune for the male Tiger and a mixed fortune for the female Tiger. There will be ample opportunities for male Tigers who are salaried workers to impress their bosses, especially in the spring and summer. Trying a career switch will bring about good results. For the self-employed who intend to go into a partnership, it is best to approach people born in the Horse or Rooster year. Money prospects are average. The prospects of female Tigers are encouraging for work matters, but she needs to take care when dealing with finances. In 2021, there could be many temptations to spend and it would certainly be in her interest to watch her money going out; otherwise this could exceed expectations. This is especially important at the 6th lunar month and end of the year, which is usually more expensive. In health, the physical discomfort you feel is caused by your moodiness due to the Mei Qi star in Ming Palace. For male Tigers, this is a good year for romance, and the best time to get married is in the summer. For the unattached female, take note: The prospects are mixed between sweet and sour. It would be best to let any new friendship form steadily, rather than rush into a hasty commitment. For the married female Tiger be careful of trouble from temptations outside the home.

Your Benefactor is: Horse
(1930, 1942, 1954, 1966, 1978, 1990, 2002, 2014)

12 Month Outlook For The Tiger

Solar Month	Comments
1st Month Feb 3rd - Mar 4th	Enjoyable peach blossom; your mate or date knows just how to keep you smiling.
2nd Month Mar 5th - Apr 3rd	Keep alert, there is a sign of anger. Strong money luck for venturing overseas.
3rd Month Apr 4th - May 4th	Average luck. Advice from friends cannot be taken at face value. Your usual good judgment is at a low.
4th Month May 5th - Jun 4th	Good luck is predicted in money matters! Substantial gain can be expected.
5th Month Jun 5th - Jul 6th	Not a beneficial time for going out late, at midnight. Be cautious of robbery.
6th Month Jul 7th - Aug 6th	Expenses for the month are uncertain. Be on guard, do not be a guarantor. Trust nobody.
7th Month Aug 7th - Sep 6th	Good in all aspects; there is something good to celebrate!
8th Month Sep 7th - Oct 7th	Auspicious money luck. Things are to your satisfaction.
9th Month Oct 8th - Nov 6th	There is a sign of conflict. Watch out for backstabbers. Silence is gold.
10th Month Nov 7th - Dec 6th	Busy month. Stress and tension could be higher than usual.
11th Month Dec 7th - Jan 4th	Focus on your health to prevent illness. Avoid overworking and relax more.
12th Month Jan 5th - Feb 3rd	Stay flexible throughout the month. Any new plans for the future requires care and consideration.

The Rabbit

Note: The New Year begins February 3rd

2021 will be a tricky year for the Rabbit. It won't necessarily be smooth or rough. Although parts of the year will go well, there are other elements that could cause problems. One of the areas of concern is the Rabbit's relations with others, and he must exercise great care with this. In particular, the Rabbit should make sure his attitude does not bring him into conflict with others and in that way jeopardize some of the good relationships he has built up. Two of the most inauspicious stars are tangling in Ming Palace, so be on guard in whatever you do, especially when signing documents. Keep your emotions aside when communicating with people and avoid acting as a guarantor for others. Career and money luck alternate between being auspicious and inauspicious. Better fortune in money luck for venturing overseas. Salaried workers should act within the confines of their abilities and try not to overestimate themselves. Your health will generally be good and there are no signs of major illnesses. In the spring and summer, an aged family member may fall ill. Avoid visiting hospitals or attending funerals. Romance is not smooth this year. Rabbits born in 1975 need to be particularly cautious of entanglement in a disastrous romance. Married couples will be emotional, and frequent quarrels may lead to separation.

Your Benefactor is: Tiger
(1938, 1950, 1962, 1974, 1986, 1998, 2010, 2022)

12 Month Outlook For The Rabbit

Solar Month	Comments
1st Month Feb 3rd - Mar 4th	Luck is average. You may frequently feel unwell or moody for no reason.
2nd Month Mar 5th - Apr 3rd	Be satisfied with small gains; don't expect too much.
3rd Month Apr 4th - May 4th	Things are average to good. Be cautious of backstabbers.
4th Month May 5th - Jun 4th	Money prospects are at their best. Make use of it.
5th Month Jun 5th - Jul 6th	Keep on high alert. There is a sign of financial loss or bleeding.
6th Month Jul 7th - Aug 6th	Auspicious luck. Conditions are stimulating you to try something new.
7th Month Aug 7th - Sep 6th	Good opportunities come your way. Daily activities and surroundings are enjoyable.
8th Month Sep 7th - Oct 7th	This is a month of conflict and tension. Signs of bleeding. Keep away from sharp objects.
9th Month Oct 8th - Nov 6th	A good time to learn something new.
10th Month Nov 7th - Dec 6th	Take care of your health. Your mood is like a bouncing ball: high and low.
11th Month Dec 7th - Jan 4th	Be conservative. Things are unstable and uncertain.
12th Month Jan 5th - Feb 3rd	This is a relatively favorable month for relationships. Lots of social opportunities and peach blossom.

The Dragon

Note: The New Year begins February 3rd

This is a moderate year. The Dragon must persist in taking the initiative and be decisive to make gain in the Ox year. Otherwise, things will go downhill. The first season of the year finds you energetically pursuing a special field of education and taking care of business interests. This could involve acquiring new skills that will further your career. It is an unusually important time. Rapid advances can be made in business and career. You can achieve great progress this year. Be level-headed when commencing new work operations; do not leave things to luck. Money luck is unstable. Cast aside any thoughts of greed if you want to prevent financial mishaps. From May 5 through June 6 avoid financial speculation of any kind. Beware of traffic accidents or injuries from sharp objects. Common health complaints for the Dragon this year are painful joints, rheumatism, and the likes. Take special care in the spring lest you dislocate a bone or joint. Where affairs of the heart are concerned, the Dragon will be quite emotional and easily fight with a loved one over trivial matter. Your most intimate personal relationship could be tense during the period from August 7 through September 6. Married couples will frequently fight over trivial matters. This may lead to someone walking away from home. Try to be more tolerant.

Your Benefactor is: Rabbit
(1939, 1951, 1963, 1975, 1987, 1999, 2011, 2023)

12 Month Outlook For The Dragon

Solar Month	Comments
1st Month Feb 3rd - Mar 4th	Average luck. Your family members may turn you from optimistic to gloomy with few hostile words.
2nd Month Mar 5th - Apr 3rd	This is the time to lay a firm foundation for the future.
3rd Month Apr 4th - May 4th	Pleasant working relationships make this a good month to launch a new project.
4th Month May 5th - Jun 4th	Cast aside any thoughts of greed if you want to prevent financial mishaps.
5th Month Jun 5th - Jul 6th	Good aspects are seen in almost everything. Long-distance business ventures are promising.
6th Month Jul 7th - Aug 6th	Auspicious luck is foreseen in money matters.
7th Month Aug 7th - Sep 6th	Backstabbers are around. You will be easily caught in squabbles.
8th Month Sep 7th - Oct 7th	You feel busy physically and mentally.
9th Month Oct 8th - Nov 6th	Luck is low. To be safe, do not visit sick people or attend funerals.
10th Month Nov 7th - Dec 6th	Watch out for sharp objects which may cause bleeding. Be alert for signs of overspending and money loss.
11th Month Dec 7th - Jan 4th	Bathe in the spring breeze! Things are so enjoyable.
12th Month Jan 5th - Feb 3rd	Relaxation is the top priority this month. Put aside all thought of work responsibilities.

The Snake

1929, 1941, 1953, 1965, 1977, 1989, 2001, 2013

Note: The New Year begins February 3rd

2021 brings good tidings to the Snake. San Tai in the Ming Palace and a brilliant money star in the Career Palace boosting the Snake's energy level and increasing the tempo of life. This enables the Snake to achieve much through tact and charm. Career and money prospects are abundant. It is also a good time to venture beyond the usual scope. You may encounter pressure and competition in work during the autumn, but luck is on your side. Though it is quite a good year, there are two inauspicious stars Guan Fu and Zhi Bei (lawsuits and backstabbing). Keep a low profile and be humble at all time. Sugarcoat your words and you should get all the cooperation you need. It is advisable for you to be on guard when signing a contract or document. Read all the fine print first and be sure you understand what it means. Think before doing anything that you know is not quite in accordance with the rules and regulations. Health-wise, apart from discomfort in your digestive system, there are no signs of major illness. The Snake's love relationship alternates between sweet and bitter this year. People around you may give you endless trouble and gossip. Though you may find a life partner, your relationship with him or her is fraught with frustration and difficulties. Married Snakes tend to get involved in a short-term romance.

Your Benefactor is: Snake
(1929, 1941, 1953, 1965, 1977, 1989, 2001, 2013)

12 Month Outlook For The Snake

Solar Month	Comments
1ˢᵗ Month Feb 3ʳᵈ - Mar 4ᵗʰ	Things go well in money and career. There is a sign of gossip. Say less and be humble.
2ⁿᵈ Month Mar 5ᵗʰ - Apr 3ʳᵈ	Things are pleasurable! Enjoy the happy moods.
3ʳᵈ Month Apr 4ᵗʰ - May 4ᵗʰ	A month of conflict. To avoid a financial mishap, do not depend on anyone.
4ᵗʰ Month May 5ᵗʰ - Jun 4ᵗʰ	Luck is noticeably moving upward. A long-distance vacation may receive unexpected benefit.
5ᵗʰ Month Jun 5ᵗʰ - Jul 6ᵗʰ	Auspicious stars are gathering. Matters turn out well in nearly all aspects.
6ᵗʰ Month Jul 7ᵗʰ - Aug 6ᵗʰ	Avoid anything secretive or underhanded.
7ᵗʰ Month Aug 7ᵗʰ - Sep 6ᵗʰ	Keep all moves simple and straightforward so that no one can accuse you of deception.
8ᵗʰ Month Sep 7ᵗʰ - Oct 7ᵗʰ	Pay attention to your health to prevent illness.
9ᵗʰ Month Oct 8ᵗʰ - Nov 6ᵗʰ	There is danger of losing a valued associate. Respond to a request whether you agree or disagree.
10ᵗʰ Month Nov 7ᵗʰ - Dec 6ᵗʰ	Conditions are easygoing and comfortable.
11ᵗʰ Month Dec 7ᵗʰ - Jan 4ᵗʰ	Things are uncertain. A wait and see attitude is the best policy.
12ᵗʰ Month Jan 5ᵗʰ - Feb 3ʳᵈ	Any ongoing negotiations should be put on hold until conditions improve.

The Horse

1930, 1942, 1954, 1966, 1978, 1990, 2002, 2014

Note: The New Year begins February 3rd

This is a mixed year for the Horse, alternating between good and bad. Money comes and money goes. Failure comes as easily as success. The first six months of the Ox year are full of gain for the Horse. However, obstacles will start appearing after July. You need to save up to prepare for uncertainties during the rest of the year. Be on guard in whatever you do from autumn onward. Mental power is good but physical energy is in short supply. Put aside tasks requiring strength and concentrate on intellectual pursuits. There are signs of financial mishap and conflict with others in September. Keep your cool in whatever you do, or you will mess things up. Come December, the Horse's luck will deteriorate even more; the only way to overcome the crisis is to be tolerant and be on your guard. Health-wise, you may suffer from allergies and minor respiratory ailments. It is advisable for you to take more rest. Romantic encounters are abundant and love relationship progress faster than expected. However, for the single Horse, if you want results, you must take the initiative. Married Horses will find it easy to have a third-party intruder in their relationship. It is especially true for Horses born in 1978. It is foreseen that a new relationship will show up for divorced Horses.

Your Benefactor is: Ox

(1937, 1949, 1961, 1973, 1985, 1997, 2009, 2021)

12 Month Outlook For The Horse

Solar Month	Comments
1st Month Feb 3rd - Mar 4th	Sunny skies! Lots of social opportunities due to strong peach blossom luck.
2nd Month Mar 5th - Apr 3rd	Watch out for cash-flow problems. Budget wisely.
3rd Month Apr 4th - May 4th	Average luck. Distant business ventures are promising.
4th Month May 5th - Jun 4th	Strong in money luck. Work hard and focus on your target; the results will be as planned
5th Month Jun 5th - Jul 6th	Good and bad mixed. Double check all your work.
6th Month Jul 7th - Aug 6th	Auspicious luck. The plans and efforts you extend will be rewarded in the future.
7th Month Aug 7th - Sep 6th	Watch out for some illness or the flu.
8th Month Sep 7th - Oct 7th	Luck is low – advice about risky investment is untrustworthy.
9th Month Oct 8th - Nov 6th	This is a good month to get married.
10th Month Nov 7th - Dec 6th	This is a favorable month for travel. A benefactor may show up.
11th Month Dec 7th - Jan 4th	This month can bring conflict and tension. Try to avoid people who aggravate you.
12th Month Jan 5th - Feb 3rd	Life moves upward. Daily activities and surroundings are easier than usual to handle.

The Sheep

Note: The New Year begins February 3rd

The Sheep conflicts with the Ox, so it will be a year of challenge and it will also be an unstable time of floating and sinking. With the Da Hao star in Ming Palace, don't expect windfalls; avoid gambling or indulging in financial speculation. The beginning of the year possibly finds you involved with personal affairs, including the fulfillment of a financial obligation. A financial matter needs attention during the spring. You are vulnerable to accidents while traveling. Be extra cautious around vehicles of all kinds. Drive defensively and be sure to use your seat belt. But if you are a Sheep born in 1979, or born in the twelfth month (around January 6 to February 3), you hold a different fortune. You can expect considerable rewards in career. Where health is concerned, you need plenty of rest to overcome mental exhaustion. Other health complaints this year are neurasthenia and ailments of the circulatory system. It will be a year of hits and miss. For the Sheep where romance is concerned. Though romantic encounters may lead to marriage, the Sheep will be quite emotional and easily fight with a loved one over trivial matter. Try your best not to nitpick or argue, otherwise, it may lead to separation. For those who are married, your spouse needs your care and understanding.

Your Benefactor is: Rat
(1936, 1948, 1960, 1972, 1984, 1996, 2008, 2020)

12 Month Outlook For The Sheep

Solar Month	Comments
1st Month Feb 3rd - Mar 4th	Be on high alert for signs of overspending or financial loss.
2nd Month Mar 5th - Apr 3rd	Stay flexible throughout the month. Carefully look for the jade among the trash.
3rd Month Apr 4th - May 4th	Money luck is at its best! Plans and effort you extend will be rewarded.
4th Month May 5th - Jun 4th	Watch out for injuries or cuts.
5th Month Jun 5th - Jul 6th	Life is busy. Stress will be higher than usual.
6th Month Jul 7th - Aug 6th	Be careful to avoid cuts and minor health problems.
7th Month Aug 7th - Sep 6th	It is likely to incur unnecessary expenditures. You will experience tense relationships with people.
8th Month Sep 7th - Oct 7th	For males, career and love are both happy, but they are frustrating for females.
9th Month Oct 8th - Nov 6th	A month filled with depression and frustration. Restrain yourself from any type of argument or fight.
10th Month Nov 7th - Dec 6th	Conflict arises easily. Say less and be humble. There are signs that gossip will tangle things up.
11th Month Dec 7th - Jan 4th	Be tolerant. Luck is mixed between good and bad.
12th Month Jan 5th - Feb 3rd	Romantic luck is strong and enjoyable.

The Monkey

1932, 1944, 1956, 1968, 1980, 1992, 2004, 2016

Note: The New Year begins February *3rd*

Last year the Monkey's luck was average. Not much excitement nor many obstacles. In the Ox year, things will be quite different. Auspicious stars Long De and Tian Xi gather in Ming Palace, enabling the Monkey to have a year of smooth sailing. Substantial rewards can be expected where career and money are concerned. The best time for you to proceed with your ambition is in the spring. However, the inauspicious stars Tian Er and Sudden Failure also mix in Ming Palace; even though your luck is extremely good, do not use underhanded ways or take short cuts to make money. If you do, you may lose everything and even worse, it may get you into trouble with the law. Those born in the sixth month (around July 7 to August 6) should be extra cautious of getting into trouble with the law over signing documents. Health-wise, avoid overworking. Common complaints are headaches and insomnia. Tian Xi celebration star shines high above, so the Monkey will have no trouble finding a prospective spouse. A fruitful relationship will come your way this autumn. Even feuding couples will kiss and make up. Married couples may have juniors to join in their love life. Those born in the sixth month (around July 7 to August 6) should stay way from liquor and undesirable liaisons.

Your Benefactor is: Pig
(1925, 1947, 1959, 1971, 1983, 1995, 2007, 2019)

12 Month Outlook For The Monkey

Solar Month	Comments
1st Month Feb 3rd - Mar 4th	A rewarding month. Most things are to your satisfaction.
2nd Month Mar 5th - Apr 3rd	Good opportunities come your way. Invest more time in your work, and the gains will be bountiful.
3rd Month Apr 4th - May 4th	Avoid believing gossip currently around you.
4th Month May 5th - Jun 4th	Lots of confusion in dealing with things. Conflict arises easily.
5th Month Jun 5th - Jul 6th	Pay attention to your health to prevent illness.
6th Month Jul 7th - Aug 6th	Be careful of sharp objects that can cause bleeding.
7th Month Aug 7th - Sep 6th	Auspicious time to offer or receive a marriage proposal!
8th Month Sep 7th - Oct 7th	Taking a business or vacation trip may produce unexpected rewards.
9th Month Oct 8th - Nov 6th	Luck is mixed. Do not be rushed into a decision that will have far-reaching effects.
10th Month Nov 7th - Dec 6th	Money luck is strong. Things will go mostly as you wish.
11th Month Dec 7th - Jan 4th	Things emerge well. Romantic encounters are plenty and totally enjoyable!
12th Month Jan 5th - Feb 3rd	Be alert for signs of overspending and money loss.

The Rooster

1933, 1945, 1957, 1969, 1981, 1993, 2005, 2017

Note: The New Year begins February 3rd

Again, the Ox year is auspicious for the Rooster after the extraordinary good fortune of 2020. The plans put into motion toward the end of last year are beginning to reap rewards for you in this year. A profitable investment opportunity will come your way in February. Career and money prospects are at their best from October 8 to November 6. However, expect setbacks and obstacles from August 7 to September 6. Be prepared for any contingency and you will go through the year without any major mishap. The salaried worker can look forward to a promotion or a change of environment in the mid-summer. For the self-employed, surprises throughout the year keep you on your toes and moving to a fast beat. Though money prospects are good, your expenditures will also rise correspondingly. Stick to what is simple and straight-forward. It is not smart to become involved in any sort of plot. Health-wise, you will experience discomfort in your digestive system and toothaches. This is a good year for courting couples to get married. Those who are single may meet their ideal life partners. A fruitful relationship awaits you this year. July 7 through August 6 and December 7 through January and into February 4 of 2022 are the best time to get married. Married Roosters born in 1981 should avoid getting involved in a love triangle.

Your Benefactor is: Rooster

(1933, 1945, 1957, 1969, 1981, 1993, 2005, 2017)

12 Month Outlook For The Rooster

Solar Month	Comments
1st Month Feb 3rd - Mar 4th	Auspicious luck. Start the work-month with a plan of attack to help you achieve long-term goals.
2nd Month Mar 5th - Apr 3rd	Good opportunities. Be ready to take advantage of a change.
3rd Month Apr 4th - May 4th	Life is busy. Be conservative and go step by step.
4th Month May 5th - Jun 4th	Take care of elderly family members. Be cautious with your own health as well.
5th Month Jun 5th - Jul 6th	Money and career have good signs, but try to prevent over-spending for no reason.
6th Month Jul 7th - Aug 6th	An auspicious time to offer or receive a marriage proposal!
7th Month Aug 7th - Sep 6th	Double-check details that others have turned over to you; their thoroughness is in doubt.
8th Month Sep 7th - Oct 7th	Do not ignore talk of a possible lawsuit. Problems may arise.
9th Month Oct 8th - Nov 6th	Money and career luck are in good sight.
10th Month Nov 7th - Dec 6th	Luck is smooth sailing. Things will go mostly as you wish.
11th Month Dec 7th - Jan 4th	Be alert for signs of overspending and money loss.
12th Month Jan 5th - Feb 3rd	Things emerge well. Romantic encounters are plenty, and everything is so enjoyable!

The Dog

1934, 1946, 1958, 1970, 1982, 1994, 2006, 2018

Note: The New Year begins February 3rd

With the auspicious stars Tian De and Fu Xing inside the Ming Palace, the Dog will have relatively good fortune in the Ox year. Career and money prospects are looking up. However, you must be on guard whatever you do and be wary of vile characters around you. Since your good fortune is not consistent, it runs quite differently from one month to another. Under the influence of Yang Ren and Jiao Sha two stars of contention, there is a strong sign of conflict with others. You are prone to temper outbursts and tend to get angry over the most trivial matter. Even worse, you may get hit by lawsuits. Keep your emotions under tight control in all situations and you will go through the year without any mishap. The self-employed will have opportunities for further development. A promotion and pay raise will come the way of salaried workers. You will be relative healthy but watch out for the flu and migraines. Those born in 1994 should refrain from climbing to high places to prevent sprains and fractures. Where affairs of the heart are concerned, you will meet several setbacks due to the Gua Su (sleep alone) star entering into your Ming Palace, so it is natural for you to feel empty and lonely. For married couples, disputes with your loved one will occur frequently. Try to be more understanding towards each other.

Your Benefactor is: Sheep
(1931, 1943, 1955, 1967, 1979, 1991, 2003, 2015)

12 Month Outlook For The Dog

Solar Month	Comments
1st Month Feb 3rd - Mar 4th	Tense relationships with people. Conflicts easily arise.
2nd Month Mar 5th - Apr 3rd	Be satisfied with small gains – don't expect too much.
3rd Month Apr 4th - May 4th	Beneficial to travel. You will have new opportunities
4th Month May 5th - Jun 4th	You may be in a low mood. Luck is mixed. Don't expect too much
5th Month Jun 5th - Jul 6th	Auspicious luck. Strong peach blossom energy (romance and social relationships) around you
6th Month Jul 7th - Aug 6th	Stay on high alert. Sweet things can turn sour.
7th Month Aug 7th - Sep 6th	Luck is low. To be safe, pay more attention to your health and do not visit sick people.
8th Month Sep 7th - Oct 7th	Luck is average. Relaxation is the top priority.
9th Month Oct 8th - Nov 6th	Career and money prospects are good. Focus on your target and work hard; the results will be what you planned.
10th Month Nov 7th - Dec 6th	Be conservative. This is an uneventful month for both career and money luck.
11th Month Dec 7th - Jan 4th	This month holds good fortune for proceeding with something new or expanding your career.
12th Month Jan 5th - Feb 3rd	Money luck is strong! All work is highly rewarded.

The Pig

1935, 1947, 1959, 1971, 1983, 1995, 2007, 2019

Note: The New Year begins February 3rd

Things will be relatively peaceful for the Pig this year except during June 5 through July 6 when there are hidden danger signs of bleeding and family members getting hit by illness. With the presence of Yi Ma, your daily life will keep busy, and it is quite beneficial for venturing overseas. Take an active stance, for example going on an overseas working trip, for it will put you in contact with some people who will benefit you and help advance your career. For the self-employed, the busier the better they are. For salaried workers, a job switch will bring good results. There are two inauspicious stars mixed in Ming Palace, one for mourning and another one brings sickness and money loss. However, financial losses can be prevented with careful judgment and budgeting wisely. Health-wise, it is possible that you may experience some disturbing symptoms, especially from Mar 5 through Apr 3, so be sure to see a doctor. Chances are there's nothing really wrong – but if there is, the quicker you get any necessary treatment, the better. With Yi Ma influencing your romance, there is a lot of vibration in the single Pig's love life. You should stay rational and refrain from being overly busy in the relationship. For married couples, your partner will complain that you don't spend enough time with him or her, and that's true.

Your Benefactor is: Monkey
(1932, 1944, 1956, 1968, 1980, 1992, 2004, 2016)

12 Month Outlook For The Pig

Solar Month	Comments
1st Month Feb 3rd - Mar 4th	Luck is average to good. Life is busy.
2nd Month Mar 5th - Apr 3rd	You feel quite flabby and dyspeptic, so avoid doing yourself harm by being overly busy.
3rd Month Apr 4th - May 4th	Energy is low. You can easily become inattentive and moody.
4th Month May 5th - Jun 4th	This is an enjoyable month for romance. An interesting relationship may lead to marriage.
5th Month Jun 5th - Jul 6th	Obligations to a friend or to a family member could be a big drain on your finances.
6th Month Jul 7th - Aug 6th	There are hidden danger signs of bleeding and family members getting hit by illness.
7th Month Aug 7th - Sep 6th	Good in money aspects, so take advantage of this month to get the financial rewards you deserve.
8th Month Sep 7th - Oct 7th	This month is blessed. There are lots of opportunities waiting at the front door.
9th Month Oct 8th - Nov 6th	Things may suddenly turn sour. Be cautious of conflicts in relationships.
10th Month Nov 7th - Dec 6th	Tian Xi star shines above; celebration enters your door. The whole month passes by happily.
11th Month Dec 7th - Jan 4th	A rewarding month. Most things are to your satisfaction.
12th Month Jan 5th - Feb 3rd	Don't expect too much. Be tolerant. You are prone to get angry over trivial matters.

The Rat

1936, 1948, 1960, 1972, 1984, 1996, 2008, 2020

Note: The New Year begins February 3rd

With Sui He in Ming Palace and Yue De shining high above in opposite Palace, the Ox year is blessed. It generally indicates that financial interests are accented at this time. This year's communications should include a few that make you very happy. They may concern anything from a much-desired social invitation, a glamorous travel opportunity, good news concerning a business deal or a wage increase, and/ or celebrating news of getting married or having a baby. Strong money luck and substantial gains can be expected by taking a long-distance journey between August 7 and September 6. However, in the following month from September 7 through October 7, there are signs of financial mishap. You are likely to incur unnecessary expenditures. There is a need to budget wisely and keep expenses under control. Be conservative and on guard in career or job changes. It is not an appropriate time to make changes. Hold your ground unless convinced that changes are necessary. Health-wise, under the influence of Bing Fu (sickness) star, you must be careful of being attacked by sudden illness. Therefore, you should stay away from places such as hospitals where contagious diseases can be found. Romance will be fruitful because of the Sui He star. There is a great opportunity for marriage. Married Rat relationships will be relatively harmonious through the year.

Your Benefactor is: Dragon
(1928, 1940, 1952, 1964, 1976, 1988, 2000, 2012)

12 Month Outlook For The Rat

Solar Month	Comments
1st Month Feb 3rd - Mar 4th	Career luck is in good view. Things come out well. Enjoyable! Things are flowing smoothly.
2nd Month Mar 5th - Apr 3rd	Focus on your target and work hard. Results will be as planned.
3rd Month Apr 4th - May 4th	Romantic luck is strong. Things are pleasurable.
4th Month May 5th - Jun 4th	Exercise more. Stay away from places such as hospitals where contagious diseases occur.
5th Month Jun 5th - Jul 6th	Be humble. There are signs of conflict and fighting.
6th Month Jul 7th - Aug 6th	Luck is neither auspicious nor inauspicious.
7th Month Aug 7th - Sep 6th	Luck is mixed. Regarding money, trust no one.
8th Month Sep 7th - Oct 7th	A month of conflict. Watch out for cash-flow problems and budget wisely.
9th Month Oct 8th - Nov 6th	Substantial gains can be expected by taking a long distance journey.
10th Month Nov 7th - Dec 6th	Auspicious stars smile on you. Don't let your good luck slips through your fingers.
11th Month Dec 7th - Jan 4th	Tense relationships with people. Gossip arises easily.
12th Month Jan 5th - Feb 3rd	Avoid excesses of any kind, such as eating, drinking, sporting, late night partying, or whatever.

感怒起于愚心蠹
而阻止於悔慎

Calligraphy by Larry Sang

Anger begins with folly
and ends in repentance.

LI MING

TABLE 1   立命   LI MING (establish fate): STEP 1: DETERMINE YOUR PALACE   立命   LI MING for 2021

This is another system for making annual predictions:

- First, use Table 1, based on your month and time of birth.
- Take the results of Table 1, and use them in Table 2, along with your year of birth, to find the palace of Li Ming for 2021
- Once you know the palace of Li Ming, read the prediction that follows for that palace.

Birth Hour:	Born After:											
	Jan 21 1st Month	Feb 19 2nd Month	Mar 20 3rd Month	Apr 20 4th Month	May 21 5th Month	Jun 21 6th Month	Jul 23 7th Month	Aug 23 8th Month	Sep 23 9th Month	Oct 23 10th Month	Nov 22 11th Month	Dec 22 12th Month
Zi 11pm–1am	Mao	Yin	Chou	Zi	Hai	Xu	You	Shen	Wei	Wu	Si	Chen
Chou 1–3am	Yin	Chou	Zi	Hai	Xu	You	Shen	Wei	Wu	Si	Chen	Mao
Yin 3–5am	Chou	Zi	Hai	Xu	You	Shen	Wei	Wu	Si	Chen	Mao	Yin
Mao 5–7am	Zi	Hai	Xu	You	Shen	Wei	Wu	Si	Chen	Mao	Yin	Chou
Chen 7–9am	Hai	Xu	You	Shen	Wei	Wu	Si	Chen	Mao	Yin	Chou	Zi
Si 9–11am	Xu	You	Shen	Wei	Wu	Si	Chen	Mao	Yin	Chou	Zi	Hai
Wu 11am–1pm	You	Shen	Wei	Wu	Si	Chen	Mao	Yin	Chou	Zi	Hai	Xu
Wei 1–3pm	Shen	Wei	Wu	Si	Chen	Mao	Yin	Chou	Zi	Hai	Xu	You
Shen 3–5pm	Wei	Wu	Si	Chen	Mao	Yin	Chou	Zi	Hai	Xu	You	Shen
You 5–7pm	Wu	Si	Chen	Mao	Yin	Chou	Zi	Hai	Xu	You	Shen	Wei
Xu 7–9pm	Si	Chen	Mao	Yin	Chou	Zi	Hai	Xu	You	Shen	Wei	Wu
Hai 9–11pm	Chen	Mao	Yin	Chou	Zi	Hai	Xu	You	Shen	Wei	Wu	Si

Notes:

These months are different from the solar (Feng Shui/Four Pillars) months, and also are different from the lunar months. They begin on the *Qi* of the *Twenty-Four Jieqi*. If born within a day of these month dates, please consult a *Ten-Thousand Year Calendar* to determine exactly which is your birth month in this system. It is not necessary for you to understand the Chinese terms in the tables. Just follow the tables to the correct palace for you.

TABLE 2 — LI MING (establish fate): STEP 2: PALACE FOR A CHOU (OX) YEAR

LI MING for 2021

Li Ming:	Rat Zi	Ox Chou	Tiger Yin	Rabbit Mao	Dragon Chen	Snake Si	Horse Wu	Sheep Wei	Monkey Shen	Rooster You	Dog Xu	Pig Hai
Birth Year:												
Zi	Hai	Zi	Chou	Yin	Mao	Chen	Si	Wu	Wei	Shen	You	Xu
Chou	Zi	Chou	Yin	Mao	Chen	Si	Wu	Wei	Shen	You	Xu	Hai
Yin	Chou	Yin	Mao	Chen	Si	Wu	Wei	Shen	You	Xu	Hai	Zi
Mao	Yin	Mao	Chen	Si	Wu	Wei	Shen	You	Xu	Hai	Zi	Chou
Chen	Mao	Chen	Si	Wu	Wei	Shen	You	Xu	Hai	Zi	Chou	Yin
Si	Chen	Si	Wu	Wei	Shen	You	Xu	Hai	Zi	Chou	Yin	Mao
Wu	Si	Wu	Wei	Shen	You	Xu	Hai	Zi	Chou	Yin	Mao	Chen
Wei	Wu	Wei	Shen	You	Xu	Hai	Zi	Chou	Yin	Mao	Chen	Si
Shen	Wei	Shen	You	Xu	Hai	Zi	Chou	Yin	Mao	Chen	Si	Wu
You	Shen	You	Xu	Hai	Zi	Chou	Yin	Mao	Chen	Si	Wu	Wei
Xu	You	Xu	Hai	Zi	Chou	Yin	Mao	Chen	Si	Wu	Wei	Shen
Hai	Xu	Hai	Zi	Chou	Yin	Mao	Chen	Si	Wu	Wei	Shen	You

Notes:

★ Take the Palace of Li Ming, found in Table 1, and compare it to the year of birth to find the palace for 2021 a Chou (Ox) year.

★ Use January 21st as the beginning of the new year for finding the birth year. If the date falls within one day of January 21st, check in a *Ten-Thousand Year Calendar* to be sure. If the birth date is between January 1st and January 20th, consider the person as belonging to the previous year in this system.

★ The predictions described below go from January 20th, 2021 until January 19th, 2022.

LI MING PALACE READING

Zi

With Sui He and Tian Yi stars shining above, financial interests are accented at this time. This should include a few things that make you very happy. Strong money luck and substantial gains can be expected. Good news concerning a business deal or a wage increase, and celebratory news of getting married may come. But under the influence of Bing Fu star, be careful of being attacked by sudden illness. Stay away from places such as hospitals where contagious diseases occur.

Chou

A year of challenge and unstable conditions. Have realistic expectations or else you will be disappointed. There is strong possibility of a job-related move or career changes. With the Hua Gai star in Ming Palace, this will be a significant year for those still in school, giving good academic results. When taking an overseas business trip, elevate your alert level to avoid conflicts with others. You may suffer financial losses or be hit by a lawsuit. Beware of traffic accidents or injuries from sharp objects.

Yin

There will be ample opportunities for salaried workers to receive raises. A career switch will bring about good results. Females need to take care when dealing with finances. There could be many temptations to avoid; otherwise she could exceed her budget and get into trouble. Even though Hong Luan star is in Ming Palace, please take note: The prospects are mixed between sweet and sour. It is not wise to rush into a hasty commitment.

Mao

Not a year to be overly optimistic. Things beyond your control could suddenly change from sweet to sour. Due to two inauspicious stars tangling in Ming Palace, be on guard in whatever you do, especially when signing documents. You must exercise great care that your attitude does not bring conflict with others. Otherwise you could ruin good relationships built up in the past. Keep your emotions aside when communicating with people and avoid acting as a guarantor for others. Take care of elderly family members. Avoid visiting hospitals or attending funerals.

LI MING PALACE READING

Chen

If Li Ming is here, you should persist in taking the initiative and be decisive in order to make substantial gains. Rapid advances can be made in business and career. The first season of the year finds you energetically pursuing a special field of education and taking care of business interests. Be level-headed when commencing new work operations; do not leave things to luck. Money luck is unstable. Cast aside any thoughts of greed if you want to prevent financial mishaps. There are signs of conflict in relationships. Do not criticize rudely when you are feeling emotional.

Si

San Tai in the Ming Palace and a brilliant money star in the Career Palace boost your energy level and increasing the tempo of life. Though it is quite a good year, there are two inauspicious stars Guan Fu and Zhi Bei (lawsuits and backstabbing). Keep a low profile and be humble at all times. To be on guard when signing a contract or document. Think before doing anything that you know is not quite in accordance with the rules and regulations. Otherwise, it is possible get entangled in legal matters.

Wu

This year alternates between good and bad. Failure comes as easily as success. An inauspicious Xiao Hao star is in Ming Palace, so money comes and money goes. You need to save to prepare for uncertainty and increased expenditures. Mental power is good but physical energy is in short supply. Put aside tasks requiring strength and concentrate on intellectual pursuits. There are signs of financial mishaps and conflict with others. Romantic encounters are abundant and love relationships progress faster than expected.

Wei

Li Ming here contains Da Hao and Sui Po, so it will be a challenging and unstable year. There is the possibility of financial mishaps related to business. Don't expect windfalls; avoid gambling or indulging in financial speculation. A financial matter needs attention during the spring. You are vulnerable to accidents while traveling. Be extra careful around vehicles of all kinds. Drive defensively. Fortunately, the De Jie star may help cancel a lot of negative qi. Plenty of rest is needed to overcome mental exhaustion.

LI MING PALACE READING

Shen

Zi Wei, Long De, and Tian Xi are in Ming Palace, therefore substantial rewards can be expected where career and money are concerned. However, Tian Er and Sudden Failure stars also mix in the Ming Palace, so do not use underhanded ways or take short cuts to make money. Otherwise, you may lose everything or even worse, it may get you into legal trouble. The celebration star Tian Xi may bring a new member to join your family; getting married or having a baby is likely.

You

With many auspicious stars around, your income will rise, and blessings will be received this year. It is predicted that the whole year is safe and sound. Salaried workers can look forward to a promotion or a change of environment. For the self-employed, surprises throughout the year keep you on your toes and keep you moving to a fast beat. Hua Gai star in Career Palace will bring good academic results for those still in school. However, be cautious; self-indulgence will bring over-consumption of many small things.

Xu

With Tian De and Fu Xing inside the Ming Palace, career and money prospects are looking up. However, your good fortune is not consistent: under the influence of Jiao Sha, a star of contention, there is a strong sign of conflict with others. Be wary of vile characters around you. Keep your emotions under tight control in all situations. The self-employed will have opportunities for further development. A promotion and pay raise will come the way of salaried workers.

Hai

With Li Ming here, things will be relatively peaceful. Because of the presence of Yi Ma, it is quite beneficial for venturing overseas. Take an active stance, like going on an overseas working trip; it will put you into contact with some beneficial people who will help advance your career. A job switch will bring good results for salaried workers. The Diao Ke star in Ming Palace is a sign of the possibility of wearing mourning clothes. Take more care of elderly family members. Avoid visiting the sick and attending funerals.

LIU REN

LIU REN (六壬)(小六壬)

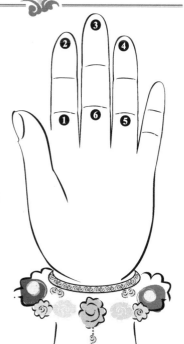

1. Great Peace
2. Back & Forth
3. Hastening Happiness
4. Red Mouth
5. Small Auspiciousness
6. Empty & Lost

Calculation:

When something out of the ordinary spontaneously happens, you can determine the meaning of the omen with *Liu Ren.*

Here is the calculation:

1. Use the left hand. Start in position 1, Great Peace (大安 da an) and always move clockwise.
2. Count clockwise through the six positions for today's *lunar* month. The Great Peace position corresponds to the first lunar month. (Refer to *Ten-Thousand Year Calendar* page at the end of this *Guide*. Find today's date, then read the month number at the top of the column).
3. Count the position found in Step 2 as the first day of the lunar month. Count clockwise through the six positions to today, the current day of the lunar month. (Find today's date in the *Ten-Thousand Year Calendar* page, then read the day number on the side at the end of the row).

4. Count the position found in Step 3 as the first double hour. Count clockwise through the six positions to the current double hour.
5. Look up the interpretation of this palace on page 44 - 45.

Hour Table

Hour	During Standard Time	During Daylight Savings Time
1	11 pm - 1 am	midnight to 2 am
2	1 - 3 am	2 - 4 am
3	3 - 5 am	4 - 6 am
4	5 - 7 am	6 - 8 am
5	7 - 9 am	8 - 10 am
6	9 - 11 am	10 - noon
7	11 am - 1 pm	noon to 2 pm
8	1 - 3 pm	2 - 4 pm
9	3 - 5 pm	4 - 6 pm
10	5 - 7 pm	6 - 8 pm
11	7 - 9 pm	8 - 10 pm
12	9 - 11 pm	10 - midnight

Note: for 11 pm to midnight during standard time, use the next day's date. For example, if it is 11:15 pm on February 12th, then count it as February 13th.

Example: July 15h, 2015, 5:30 pm

A. Start in Position One.
B. July 15th is in the column that says 5th month at the top. So we go to Position Two.
C. July 15th is the 30th day of the 5th month.
D. Start where we left off in Position Five and call that 1. Count clockwise to the 30th position from there: Position Four.
E. Start in Position Four and count for the hour.
F. During Daylight Savings Time, 5:30 pm is the 10th hour. Count 10 positions, with Position Four and call that 1, and end up in Position Two.

This is the outcome:

Position Two is **Back and Forth**
Read the interpretation on the next page and apply it to the situation.

Interpretation

1. Great Peace (大安 da an):

The person in question has not moved at this time. This position belongs to Wood element and the East. Generally in planning matters, use 1, 5, and 7. This position belongs to the four limbs. Helpful people are found in the Southwest. Avoid the East. Children, women and the six domestic animals are frightened.

In Great Peace, every activity prospers. Seek wealth in the Southwest. Lost items are not far away. The house is secure and peaceful. The person you expect has not left yet. Illness is not serious. Military generals return home to the fields. Look for opportunities and push your luck.

2. Back and Forth (留連 liu lian):

The person you expect is not returning yet. This position belongs to Water element and the North. Generally in planning matters, use 2, 8, and 10. This position belongs to the kidneys and stomach. Helpful people are found in the South. Avoid the North. Children wander the road as disembodied spirits.

With Back and Forth, activities are difficult to achieve. You have not adequately planned for your goals. Official activities are delayed. Those who have gone do not return from their journey yet. Lost items appear in the South. Hurry and ask for what you want and you will get results. But guard against gossip and disputes. Family members for the moment are so-so.

3. Hastening Happiness (速喜 su xi):

The expected person arrives shortly. This position belongs to Fire element and the South. Generally in planning matters, use 3, 6, and 9. This position belongs to the heart and brain. Helpful people are found in the Southwest. Avoid the South. Children, women, and animals are frightened.

With Hastening Happiness, happiness arrives. Seek wealth toward the South. Lost items are found between 11 am and 5 pm if you ask a passerby about it. Official activities have blessing and virtue. Sick people have no misfortune. Auspicious for the fields, house, and the six livestock. You receive news from someone far away.

4. Red Mouth (赤口 chi kou)

An inauspicious time for official activities. This position belongs to Metal element and the West. Generally in planning matters, use 4, 7, and 10. This position belongs to the lungs and stomach. Helpful people are found in the East. Avoid the West. Children are bewildered young spirits.

Red Mouth governs quarrels and disputes. Be cautious about legal matters. Quickly go search for lost items. Travelers experience a fright. The six domestic animals give you trouble. The sick should go to the West. Furthermore, you must guard against being cursed. Fear catching epidemic diseases.

5. Small Auspiciousness (小吉 xiao ji)

The expected person comes in a happy time. This person belongs to Wood element and all directions. Generally in planning matters, use 1, 5, and 7. This position belongs to the liver and intestines. Helpful people are found in the Southwest. Avoid the East. Children, women and the six domestic animals are frightened.

Small Auspiciousness is most auspicious and prosperous. Your road is smooth. Spirits come announcing good news. Lost items are located in the Southwest. Travelers promptly arrive. Relations with others are extremely strong. Everything is harmonious. A sick person should pray to heaven.

6. Empty and Lost (空亡 kong wang)

News you expect does not come at this time. This position belongs to Earth element. Generally in planning matters, use 3, 6, and 9. This position belongs to the spleen and brain. Helpful people are found in the North. Watch out for the health of your children. Males feel pressure. The activities of females get no results.

Spirits are often unreasonable or perverse. Seeking wealth is without benefit. There is disaster for travelers. Lost items will not appear. Official activities bring punishment and damage. Sick people meet a dark ghost. To be secure and peaceful, get release from calamity by sacrifice and prayer.

Example: You arrive at the airport, but your ride is late to pick you up. You use Liu Ren to find out what is going on.

Today's time and date: May 10th, 2015, 2:30 pm

A. Start in Position One.

B. May 10th is in the column that says 3rd month at the top.
   So we go to Position Three.
   May 10th is the 22nd day of the 3rd month.
   Start where we left off in Position Three and call that 1.

C. Count clockwise to the 22nd position from there: Position Six.
   Start in Position Six and count for the hour.
   Standard Time, 2:30 pm is the 8th hour.

D. Count 8 positions, with Position Six as the beginning, and end up in Position One.

This is the outcome:

Position Three is **Great Peace**
Read the text and apply it to the situation. Great Peace begins with "The person you expect has not left yet." Your flight had arrived early. You wait calmly for 30 minutes and your ride arrives, at what would've been on time.

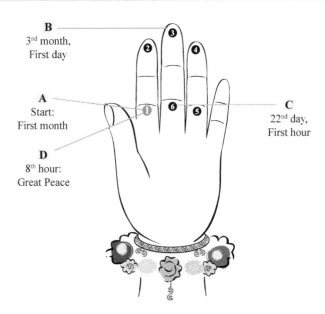

B
3nd month,
First day

A
Start:
First month

C
22nd day,
First hour

D
8th hour:
Great Peace

OMEN

OMENS

In Chinese almanacs, there are often listings of predictions based on omens. We include a few below. Have fun with it and don't take it too seriously.

Omens from the Twitch of an Eye

Time	Eye	This is an omen of:
11 pm - 1 am Zi	Left	Meeting a benefactor
	Right	Having a good meal
1 - 3 am Chou	Left	Having anxiety
	Right	Someone thinking about you
3 - 5 am Yin	Left	Someone coming from afar
	Right	A happy matter arriving
5 - 7 am Mao	Left	The coming of an important guest
	Right	Something peaceful, safe and auspicious
7 - 9 am Chen	Left	A guest coming from afar
	Right	Injury or harm
9 - 11 am Si	Left	Having a good meal
	Right	Something inauspicious
11 am - 1 pm Wu	Left	Having a good meal
	Right	An inauspicious matter
1 - 3 pm Wei	Left	A lucky Star
	Right	Good luck, but small
3 - 5 pm Shen	Left	Money coming
	Right	Someone thinking of you romantically
5 - 7 pm You	Left	A guest coming
	Right	A guest arriving
7 - 9 pm Xu	Left	A guest arriving
	Right	A gathering or meeting
9 - 11 pm Hai	Left	A guest arriving
	Right	Gossip

Correct for *Daylight Savings Time*, if in use (subtract one hour from the current time).

Omens from Hiccoughs

Time	This is an omen of:
11 pm - 1 am Zi	A good meal and a happy dinner gathering
1 - 3 am Chou	Someone missing you; a guest coming to seek your help
3 - 5 am Yin	Someone missing you; a dining engagement
5 - 7 am Mao	Wealth and happiness; someone coming to ask about a matter
7 - 9 am Chen	A good meal; great good luck for everyone
9 - 11 am Si	A lucky person coming to seek wealth
11 am - 1 pm Wu	An important guest; someone wanting a dinner gathering
1 - 3 pm Wei	Someone wanting a meal; lucky activities
3 - 5 pm Shen	Nightmares; eating is not beneficial
5 - 7 pm You	Someone coming; someone asks about a matter
7 - 9 pm Xu	Someone missing you; a meeting brings benefit
9 - 11 pm Hai	Something frightens, but on the contrary, brings benefit

Correct for *Daylight Savings Time*, if in use (subtract one hour from the current time).

True faith and
courage
are like kites:
An opposing
wind
lifts them
higher.

真正信心就像風箏，
逆風才飛得更高

Calligraphy by Larry Sang

THE YELLOW EMPEROR

THE YELLOW EMPEROR
IN THE FOUR SEASONS

黃帝四季詩

SPRING

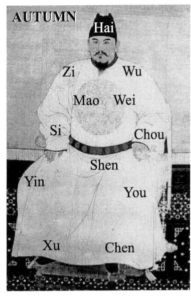

AUTUMN

SUMMER

WINTER

52

There is a lifetime prediction commonly found in Chinese almanacs. Based on your season of birth, find your birth time.

The Yellow Emperor in the Four Seasons

Time of Birth		Season of Birth			
		Spring February 4th to May 4th	**Summer** May 5th to August 6th	**Autumn** August 7th to November 6th	**Winter** November 7th to February 3rd
Zi	11p-1a	head	low abdomen	shoulders	low abdomen
Chou	1-3a	chest	hands	hands	knees
Yin	3-5a	feet	feet	knees	chest
Mao	5-7a	shoulders	shoulders	chest	shoulders
Chen	7-9a	knees	knees	feet	feet
Si	9-11a	hands	hands	hands	head
Wu	11a-1p	low abdomen	head	shoulders	hands
Wei	1-3p	hands	chest	chest	knees
Shen	3-5p	feet	feet	low abdomen	chest
You	5-7p	shoulders	shoulders	knees	shoulders
Xu	7-9p	knees	knees	feet	feet
Hai	9-11p	chest	chest	head	hands

Correct birth time for Daylight Saving Time, if used at the time of birth. If you were born in the Southern Hemisphere, switch the autumn and spring dates, as well as the summer and winter dates.

The Yellow Emperor in the Four Seasons

Born on the Yellow Emperor's Head means a lifetime of never having worries. Even petty people have riches and honor. Clothes and food naturally come around. Your position in society is elevated, and gentlemen are good at planning. Women go through life steadily and smoothly, marrying a talented and educated person.

Born on the Yellow Emperor's Hands means business capital is sufficient. Going out, you meet a benefactor. Inside the home, you have everything. Your early years are very steady and smooth. You accumulate many possessions. Wealth comes from every direction. When old, it is in your hands.

The Yellow Emperor in the Four Seasons

Born on the Yellow Emperor's Shoulders means a life of a million riches. You have wealth in your middle years. Children and grandchildren are plenty. Clothes and income at all times are good. In old age, you have fields in the village. Siblings are helpful. Your early life is bitter, but the later end is sweet.

Born on the Yellow Emperor's Chest means clothes and food are naturally ample. Experts in the pen and the sword are around you. There is music, song, and dance. Middle age brings good clothes and food. Later years are happy and prosperous. Joy, utmost honor, prosperity, and increased longevity add more blessings.

Born on the Yellow Emperor's Lower Abdomen, you were treasured by your parents. In middle age, clothes and food are good. When old you obtain gold. The family reputation is changing a lot. You are a noble person. Children and grandchildren must newly shine. Cultured and bright, they advance a lot.

Born on the Yellow Emperor's Knees means doing things is without benefit. In your early years, you toiled a lot, but did not lack clothes and food. Everyday, you travel on the road; you cannot avoid running back and forth. Old age is smooth, with honor and prosperity, but in middle age, hard work is extreme.

Born on the Yellow Emperor's Feet, practice moral teachings to avoid toil. A lifetime that is safe and sound, but unsuitable to reside in your ancestor's home. Women marry two husbands. Men have two wives. Search lonely mountain ranges. Leave your homeland to achieve good fortune.

FENG SHUI

FENG SHUI

Makes the Universe Work for You

 We live in a universe that is filled with different energies. Our planet rotates on its axis, creating cycles of day and night. The Earth also revolves around the sun in yearly cycles and is subject to various gravitational and magnetic fields. Our solar system is moving through space and is also subject to other forces in the universe. These physical forces and many different time cycles affects us profoundly. The Chinese have spent centuries observing the effects with their environment. This is the science and art of Feng Shui (Chinese geomancy).

Feng Shui uses observation, repeatable calculations and methodologies, and is based on the study of the environment, both inside and out of the house. Feng Shui can help you determine the best home to live in, which colors can enhance your home, the best bed positions for deep sleep, and how to change your business or home into a center of power. Feng Shui can help improve your health, your relationships and your prosperity. It is based on a complex calculation and observation of the environment, rather than a metaphysical reading relying on inspiration or intuition.

The American Feng Shui Institute publishes the annual Chinese Astrology and Feng Shui Guide so that both the Feng Shui professional and layperson can benefit from the knowledge of the incoming energy cycles and their influences. With this knowledge, one can adjust their environment to make it as harmonious as possible for the current year.

The following Sections contain the energy patterns for the current year with an analysis and remedy for each of the eight directions. For the nonprofessional, there is a Section on how to prepare your home for this reading. Please note that Feng Shui is a deep and complex science that requires many years to master. Preparing your home to receive the annual energy is one aspect that anyone can apply. A professional reading is recommended to anyone who wishes to receive the greatest benefits possible that Feng Shui can bring.

Preparing your home for a Feng Shui reading

The Floor Plan

The first requirement for preparing your home for a Feng Shui annual reading is to create a proportional floor plan. This plan can be hand drawn or be the original building plans, as long as the plan is proportionally correct. It is not necessary to draw in all your furniture except perhaps noting your bed and desk. It is important that you indicate where all window and door openings are.

Example B
Floor Plan

Example A
Floor Plan

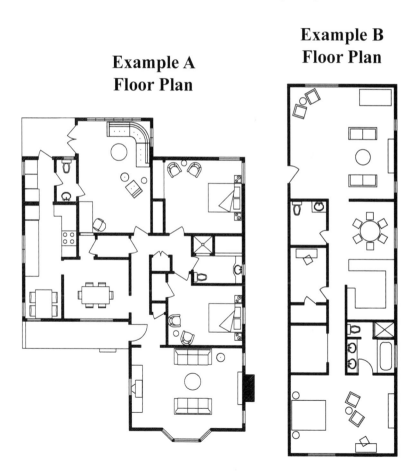

Preparing your home for a Feng Shui reading

Gridding The Floor Plan

Once you have your floor plan drawn, you then overlay a 9 - square grid. This grid is proportional to the floor plan. If it were a long and narrow house, so would the grid be long and narrow. You want to divide the floor plan into equal thirds both top to bottom and left to right as shown below:

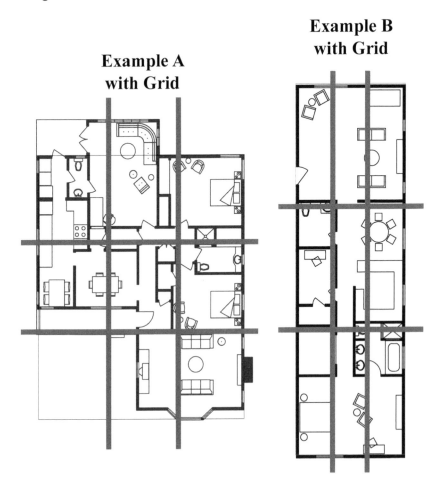

Example A
with Grid

Example B
with Grid

The Compass Reading

The next step is to determine the alignment of your house with the Earth magnetic fields by taking a compass reading. It is very important to take an accurate reading and not guess the orientation based on the direction of the sun or a map.

Why Do You Need To Use A Compass?

In Feng Shui, we look at the eight cardinal and inter-cardinal directions: East, Southeast, South, Southwest, West, Northwest, North, and Northeast when analyzing a home or building. Each of these directions hold unique significance to these building. If you do not use a compass to determine the correct orientation, you might completely misread your home. You cannot map the Qi within the building without an exact orientation. It is similar to finding your way out of a forest without a compass. You have a high probability of getting lost. Without a compass, it simply is not Feng Shui.

A Compass vs A Luopan

You can use any compass if you do not have a Luopan. The Luopan is simply a Chinese compass that helps determine the sitting direction of a building. It also contains a wealth of information on its dial that is used for more advanced applications. In recent years, Master Larry Sang simplified the traditional Luopan specifically for training Western students. Although it looks simple compared to an original Luopan, it has all the tools you need to accurately analyze a building. An important fact to remember about a Luopan is that it points to the South. The following information and instructions apply to a Luopan, however, if you are using a Western compass these concepts are easy to adapt.

SANG'S LUOPAN

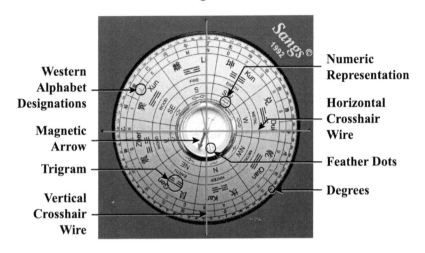

Western Alphabet Designations

Magnetic Arrow

Trigram

Vertical Crosshair Wire

Numeric Representation

Horizontal Crosshair Wire

Feather Dots

Degrees

Parts of Sang's Luopan

The Magnetic Arrow - The arrowhead points South rather than North. Western compasses point North.

The Feather Dots - (The twin dots at the center of the rotating dial). Always adjust the rotating (gold) dial to align the twin dots with the feather end of the arrow.

The Numeric Representations - The innermost ring has a dot pattern that represents the Trigram' numbers. For example Kun has two dots and Qian has six dots.

Crosshair Alignments - The red crosshairs designate the facing and sitting directions. Once the arrow is steady and the feather end is aligned over the North twin dots, you can determine the sitting direction and the facing direction.

The Eight Trigrams - The Eight Trigrams are the basis for orientation in Feng Shui and are shown on the Luopan with their perspective elements, symbols, and directions.

Western Alphabet Designations - Each Trigram is divided into three equal parts. These parts are shown with both their Chinese symbols and using the Western Alphabet.

The Degrees - Outermost on the dial are the Western compass degree in Arabic numerals.

General Guidelines for using the Luopan:

To use the Luopan or compass correctly, remember the following guidelines:

1. Always stand straight and upright.

2. Do not wear Metal jewelry or belt buckles that can skew the compass.

3. Avoid any electrical influences such as automobiles or electrical boxes.

4. Always stand parallel to the building.

5. Keep your feet square below you.

6. You can keep the Luopan in the lower box case to manage it better.

Taking a reading with the Luopan:

With the general guidelines for using a luopan in mind, now you ar ready to take a reading to determine which wall or corner of your home is located closest to the North.

1. Take your reading outside, standing parallel to your home with your back to it. Stand straight and hold the Luopan at waist level. Wait until the arrow ceases to quiver.

2. Slowly turn the center (gold) dial so that the North/feather dots aligh with the feather of the arrow. If using a Western compass, turn the compass so that the needle's arrow end aligns with North (between 337.5º - 22.5º).

3. Please take at lEast three separate readings from other positions. If you find that there is a discrepancy, take various readings at various locations until you are sure which one is correct. One direction should stand out as being correct.

4. Indicate on your floor plan which Section is North. Fill in the other directions as illustrated. Please note that North can lie in a corner Section.

Example B

Example A

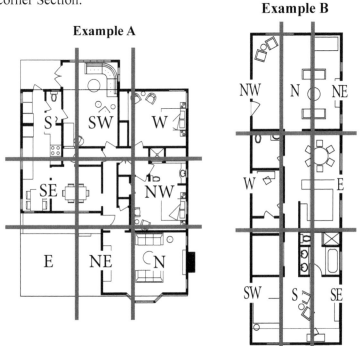

DIRECTIONS TO AVOID
FOR CONSTRUCTION 2021

The Three Sha, Sui Po, and Tai Sui

The **Three Sha** are in the **East: Yin, Mao, and Chen** directions.
The **Sui Po** or **Year Breaker** is in the
Southwest: Wei direction.
The **Tai Sui** is in the
Northeast: Chou direction.

Therefore, avoid using these directions:
Chou, Yin, Mao, Chen, and Wei

Directions to Avoid

15° Direction	Degrees	45° Direction	Sang's Luopan Alpha Designation
Chou		NE	c
Yin			e
Jia	22.5° - 127.5°	E	f
Mao			g
Yi			h
Chen		SE	i
Wei	202.5°-217.5°	SW	o

What should we avoid in these directions?

- New construction sitting in these directions (except Chou Northeast).
- Major renovation to buildings sitting in these directions (except Chou Northeast).
- Major renovation to this section of the house, regardless of the sitting direction.
- Burial of the deceased in these directions.
- Digging or breaking of earth in these directions. If digging cannot be avoided in any of these areas, then place a metal wind chime outside between the house and the digging site.
- In addition, Ox or Sheep born in the third, sixth, nine or twelfth month of the lunar calendar should avoid attending funerals or burials.

FENG SHUI

2021

The Qi (energy) shift begins on
February 3rd at 11:08 p.m.

SE ▦ **5** Yellow	**S** ▦ **1** White	**SW** ▦ **3** Jade
E ▦ **4** Green	**6** White	**W** ▦ **8** White
NE ▦ **9** Purple	**N** ▦ **2** Black	**NW** ▦ **7** Red

Qi Pattern

INTRODUCTION

While this diagram may look foreign to the beginner, it is essential information for the experienced Feng Shui practitioner. Each year the Qi pattern brings different effects. Some of these effects are quite auspicious and favorable and some may be inauspicious and not so favorable.

The effects of the 2021 energy pattern are analyzed for you in the following pages. Each analysis contains suggested remedies or enhancements for each Section. Remedies are recommended to reduce negative Qi. Enhancements are recommended to increase beneficial Qi. These remedies or enhancements consist of the five elements: Wood, Fire, Earth, Metal, and Water.

To use a remedy or enhancement, it must be placed inside the house within that particular Section. If more than one room exists within a Section, then each room needs to have its own remedy or enhancement. Any exceptions will be noted.

Feng Shui

FENG SHUI ❧ 2021

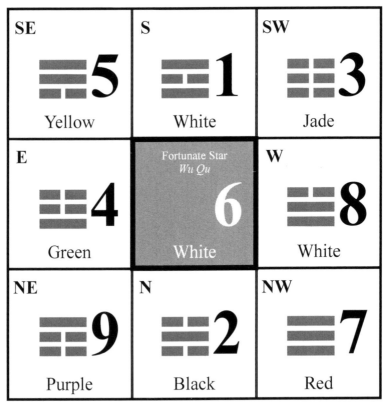

SE	S	SW
☴ **5**	☵ **1**	☷ **3**
Yellow	White	Jade
E	Fortunate Star *Wu Qu*	W
☳ **4**	**6**	☶ **8**
Green	White	White
NE	N	NW
☲ **9**	☴ **2**	☰ **7**
Purple	Black	Red

The Center Section

Center

Analysis:

Last year (2020), the 7 Po Jun Star visited the center. We are currently in Period 8. The 8 White Star is earth element, so it strengthened the Po Jun Star's metal qi. The 7 Po Jun Star is a competitive fighting star. Therefore, we predicted the world would enter another time of "growth of fighting and conflict." Economic recovery might be slow and painful due to the Po Jun Star (metal element) reducing the center qi of the 8 White Wealth Star.

This year the 6 Fortunate Wu Qu Star is in the center, it will be more unfavorable than the last year, the Rat year. The Wu Qu star also is metal element, so we can predict that 2021 will not be a peaceful year. The worldwide economic crisis still lies ahead, and we will see the start of currency wars and trade wars. Meanwhile, people may experience fighting, fire-related disasters such as forest fires, corruption exposed in political circles, and people protesting all over the world. Real estate in US will continue to fall. Chinese property prices will drop 30 to 45% overall.

Feng Shui

FENG SHUI

2021

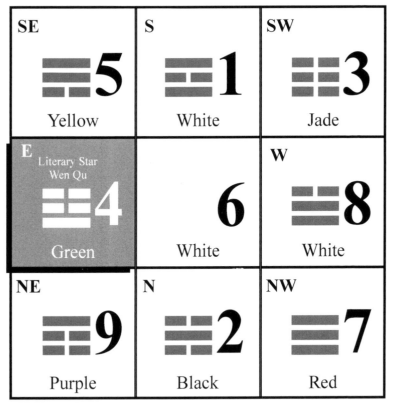

SE ䷸ **5** Yellow	**S** ䷸ **1** White	**SW** ䷸ **3** Jade
E Literary Star Wen Qu ䷸ **4** Green	**6** White	**W** ䷸ **8** White
NE ䷸ **9** Purple	**N** ䷸ **2** Black	**NW** ䷸ **7** Red

The East Section

East

Situation:
Doors, bedrooms, study rooms in the east section.

Analysis:
The 4 Green Wen Qu Literary Star is in the east in 2021. The Literary Star represents creative and academic achievements and Peach Blossom. Its element is wood. The east section is the home of the 3 Jade Lu Cun Star, which is also wood element. Since wood and wood are the same element, it creates a strong relationship. Make use of the east section to benefit business expansion and bring strong romance (peach blossom) qi. This section is beneficial for literature, scholars, writers, artists, sales, students, and people in entertainment industry.

To make full use of it: Fire
Fire element possibilities include a red light bulb, a lamp with red shade or any decorative item with the red color. One can also use corresponding colors such as maroon, purple, or fuchsia. Actual fire, such as burning candles, are not recommended.

Caution:
Strong Peach Blossom. One can easily encounter extramarital affairs.

Feng Shui

FENG SHUI ❧ 2021

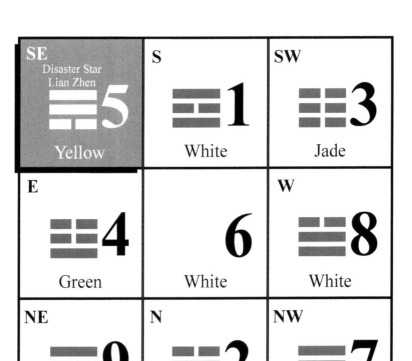

SE Disaster Star Lian Zhen ☷ **5** Yellow	**S** ☵ **1** White	**SW** ☴ **3** Jade
E ☴ **4** Green	**6** White	**W** ☶ **8** White
NE ☳ **9** Purple	**N** ☴ **2** Black	**NW** ☰ **7** Red

The Southeast Section

Southeast

Situation:
Doors, bedrooms, study rooms in the southeast section.

Analysis:
The 5 Yellow Lian Zhen Disaster Star visits the southeast this year. This star is also called the 5 Yellow Sha and Evil Influence Star or the Yellow Pestilence Star. It brings potential delays, obstacles, fires, lawsuits, sickness, and casualty. The 5 Yellow Star is earth element. The Southeast is the home position of the 4 Green Wen Qu Star; its element is wood. Wood and metal have a domination relationship. Therefore, if your bedroom falls in this section, the potential to develop tumors can exist if a remedy is not applied. However, it is advisable to avoid staying or spending a lot of time in this area. It is also critically important not to do ground-breaking or construction in this section, since it is easy to arouse misfortune.

Remedy: Metal
To reduce the potential of the above-mentioned negative effects, use a metal remedy in this section. The metal can be a decorative metal sculpture or ornament. An ornament which has moving metal parts is preferable, such as grandfather clock.

Caution:
Do not do construction or dig in the earth.

FENG SHUI ❧ 2021

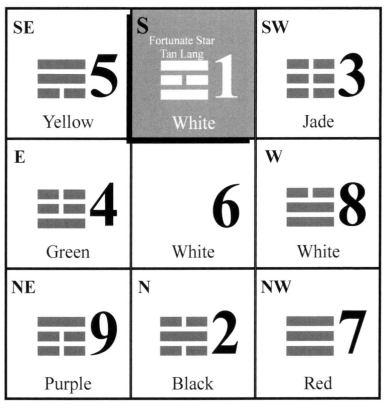

SE	S	SW
☴ **5** Yellow	**Fortunate Star Tan Lang** ☱ **1** White	☷ **3** Jade
E ☳ **4** Green	**6** White	**W** ☰ **8** White
NE ☲ **9** Purple	**N** ☵ **2** Black	**NW** ☶ **7** Red

The South Section

South

Situation: Doors, bedrooms, study rooms in the south section.

Analysis:
The 1 White Tan Lang Fortunate Star is in the south section this year. This Fortunate Star represents wealth, fame, romance, and good negotiation skills. The element of the 1 White Star is water. The south is home to the 9 Purple Star which brings promotions and celebration. Though the nature of the 1 White Tan Lang Fortunate Star and the 9 Purple Star are auspicious, yet the south sector is the base of fire element. Water and fire create a disharmonious domination relationship. This Ox year, one should avoid construction and digging in the south section. Otherwise, some unhappy things, such as casualties, bleeding, heart attack, gunshot wounds, or fire-related disasters are easily aroused.

Caution:
Don't do construction or dig in the ground.
Not beneficial for jewelry, goldsmiths, or metal-related businesses.

Remedy: Plants
Use indoor plants to remedy the disharmonious domination relationship.

After Remedy:
Beneficial for people in love to march toward the wedding chapel.

Feng Shui

FENG SHUI

2021

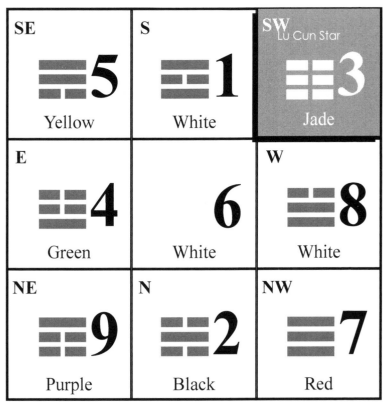

SE 5 Yellow	S 1 White	SW Lu Cun Star 3 Jade
E 4 Green	6 White	W 8 White
NE 9 Purple	N 2 Black	NW 7 Red

The Southwest Section

Southwest

Situation: Doors, bedrooms, study rooms in the southwest section.

Analysis:
In 2021 the 3 Jade Lu Cun Star visits the southwest. The 3 Jade Lu Cun Star is wood element. It is a star of fighting, robberies, arguments, misunderstandings, and gossip. The southwest section is the home of 2 Black Ju Men Star, whose element is earth. Wood and earth have dominating relationship, which creates disharmony in the family, especially for a housewife. Therefore, if spending a lot of time in southwest, you should be cautious of health problems or sexually transmitted diseases. Moreover, this year with an inauspicious star called Sudden Failure in the Southwest, it is not advisable for doing any construction or ground-breaking here, as misfortune from sickness or robbery is easily aroused.

Caution:
Don't do construction or ground digging. Not beneficial for housewives or elderly women to stay in this section as the master bedroom.

Remedy: Fire
To reduce the above-mentioned potential negative effects. A possible fire element can be a red light bulb or a lamp with red shade or any decorative item with the red color or its corresponding colors of maroon, purple, or fuchsia.

FENG SHUI 2021

SE ☴ 5 Yellow	**S** ☲ 1 White	**SW** ☷ 3 Jade
E ☳ 4 Green	6 White	**W** Money Star Zuo Fu ☶ 8 White
NE ☶ 9 Purple	**N** ☵ 2 Black	**NW** ☰ 7 Red

The West Section

West

Situation:
Doors, bedrooms, study rooms in the west section.

Analysis:
This year the 8 White Zuo Fu Wealth Star arrives in the west. The 8 White Star is earth element and is at its strongest time in the current Period 8. West is the home of the 7 Red Po Jun Star which is metal element. These two stars, earth and metal, have a productive relationship, and moreover an auspicious money star named Lu Cun makes this section one of the most auspicious ones to use in 2021. It can produce good money luck, fame, and new developments or breakthroughs. Spending time here will be beneficial for new development, breakthroughs, wealth, and promotions.

Benefits:
Beneficial for new development, expansion, and breakthroughs.Prosperous for land developers, real estate agents, jewelry business, goldsmiths, and other metal-related business

Enhancement: Earth
Use earth element. This can be a decorative piece of glazed pottery or porcelain.

FENG SHUI

2021

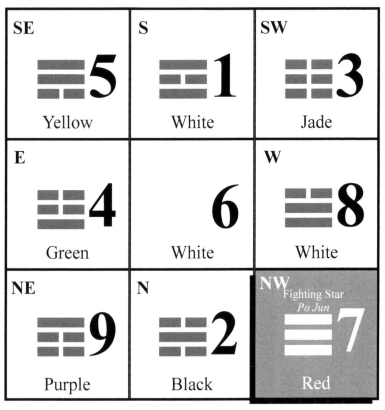

SE 5 Yellow	**S** 1 White	**SW** 3 Jade
E 4 Green	6 White	**W** 8 White
NE 9 Purple	**N** 2 Black	**NW** Fighting Star *Po Jun* 7 Red

The Northwest Section

Northwest

Situation:
Doors, bedrooms, study rooms in the northwest section.

Analysis:
This year the 7 Red Po Jun Fighting Star is in the northwest. The 7 Po Jun Star is a competitive and fighting star. The 7 Red Star's element is metal. Northwest is the home of the 6 White Fortune Star which is also metal element. Metal plus more metal easily create a conflict. If the main entrance or bedroom falls in this section, be careful of conflicts with others, mostly due to challenging the power of authority. Also, be on guard for unexpected harm, such as gunshot wounds, bleeding, or financial losses.

Caution:
Be on guard for unexpected harm, such as gunshot wounds, bleeding, and financial losses.

Remedy: Water
Use water element, for example a water fountain, aquarium, or the colors of blue or black.

Feng Shui

FENG SHUI

2021

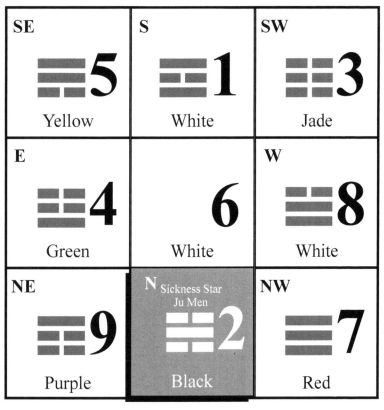

SE ▤**5** Yellow	**S** ▤**1** White	**SW** ▤**3** Jade
E ▤**4** Green	**6** White	**W** ▤**8** White
NE ▤**9** Purple	**N** Sickness Star Ju Men ▤**2** Black	**NW** ▤**7** Red

The North Section

North

Situation:
Doors, bedrooms, study rooms in the north section.

Analysis:
The 2 Black Ju Men Star is in the north section this year. The 2 Black Ju Men Star is earth element, it represents sickness, gossip, and misunderstandings. The north is the home of the 1 White Fortune Star and it is water element. The 2 Black Ju Men Star (earth element) and the 1 White (water element) have a domination relationship. In 2021, the Bing Fu Sickness Inauspicious Star is located in the north, so if spending a lot of time in this section, you should watch out for health problems, sexually transmitted diseases, and unfavorable legal affairs.

Caution:
Not beneficial for pregnant or elderly women to stay in this area.

Remedy: Metal
To reduce the potential for the above-mentioned negative effects, use metal element as a remedy in this section. The remedy can consist of decorative metal décor such as a piece of sculpture or an ornament. Something with moving metal parts is preferable, such as a grandfather clock.

Feng Shui

FENG SHUI

2021

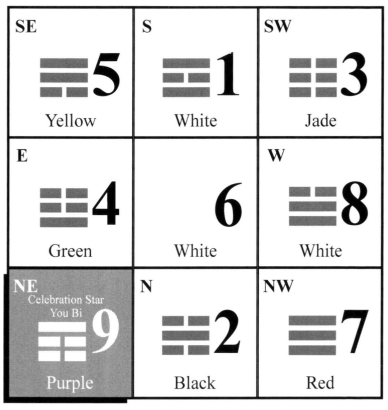

SE ▤ **5** Yellow	**S** ▤ **1** White	**SW** ▤ **3** Jade
E ▤ **4** Green	**6** White	**W** ▤ **8** White
NE Celebration Star You Bi ▤ **9** Purple	**N** ▤ **2** Black	**NW** ▤ **7** Red

The Northeast Section

Northeast

Situation:
Doors, bedrooms, study rooms in the northeast section.

Analysis:
The 9 Purple You Bi Celebration Star is in the northeast this year. This 9 Purple Star represents wealth, promotions, romance, and celebration. Its element is fire. The northeast belongs to the 8 White Zuo Fu Money Star and brings fame and wealth. Its element is earth. The 9 Purple (fire) and the 8 White (earth) have a productive relationship. This makes the northeast one of the most beneficial sections for the year of the Ox (2021). Fire provides strong energy to earth element, so this becomes a celebration and wealth-making section. This combination brings renown, wealth, and is excellent for money prospects. It is also good for students to pass tests and for romance. People should make use of this area more often.

Benefits:
Beneficial for politicians, merchants, students, and married couples looking for a baby. It is prosperous for land developers and real estate agents.

Enhancement: Fire
Use fire element in this section. An enchancement can be any red decorative item or its corresponding colors of maroon, purple, or fuchsia.

最貧窮的不是身無分文，而是沒有夢想

Calligraphy by Larry Sang

The poorest one is not one without a cent,
but one without a dream.

DAY SELECTION

DAY SELECTION

Introduction to Day Selection

Day Selection has been used for a long time in China. Every year, almanacs would be published giving the best days for important activities, as well as days to avoid. It is thought that a positive outcome is more likely when an activity is begun on an auspicious day. In English, we talk abut getting things off to a good Start, but have no particular methodology to do this.

There are three aspects to selecting a good day: picking a day that is good for the activity, avoiding a day that is bad for the activity, and picking a day that is not bad for the person(s) involved. In the calendar pages that follow, each day will list two or three activities that are auspicious or inauspicious on that day. If you wanted to pick a date to get married, you would first look for the days that were considered good for weddings. In addition, you need to check the birth information of the bride and groom. If the bride is a Rabbit and the groom is a Rat, then you also need to avoid any days that say Bad for Rat or Bad for Rabbit, even if they are good for weddings in general.

In addition, there are some days that are not good for any important activity. Usually this is because the energy of heaven and Earth is too strong or inharmonious on those days.

Day Selection is used for the first day of an activity. It does not affect a continued activity. For example, you should begin construction on a day that is good for ground breaking, but it is not a problem if the construction is continued through a day that is bad for ground breaking. The construction need not be stopped.

On the next page are definitions of the various activities included in Master Sang's Day Selection Calendar.

CALENDAR TERMINOLOGY KEY

Animals:
Generally a bad day for a person born in the year of the animal listed. Even if an activity is listed as beneficial for that day, it will usually not be beneficial for that animal.

*Begin Mission:
Beginning a new position, mission, or assignment.

Burial:
Burial.

*Business:
Trade or business.

*Buy Property:
Purchasing real estate.

*Construction:
Begin work on buildings, roads, etc.

*Contracts:
Signing or entering into a contract, commitment, or agreement.

Don't Do Important Things:
A bad day for most activities.

Fix House:
Repairing the inside or outside of the house. Also for installing major appliances, such as the stove or oven.

Funeral:
Funerals.

*Grand Opening:
Opening a new business, restaurant, etc. Opening ceremonies for a new event.

Ground Breaking:
Beginning construction or disturbing the Earth.

Ground Digging:
Unearth or excavate the Earth with a shovel or spade to remove material or plants.

Hunting:
To chase wild animals for the purpose of catching or killing.

Lawsuit:
Filing a lawsuit or going to court.

*Moving:
Moving or changing residences.

Planting:
Gardening or planting.

Prayer:
Praying for blessings or happiness.

School:
Admissions into a new school.

Surgery:
Medical treatment or operation.

*Travel:
Going out or beginning a trip.

*Wedding:
Marriage ceremonies or becoming engaged to be married.

Worship:
Rituals, rites, ceremonies, offering sacrifices, or honoring ancestors or the dead.

Most Activities:
Includes all activities marked. (*)

January 2021

Unfavorable for:

Day	Details	Unfavorable
Fri **1**	**Good for:** prayer, house cleaning ***Bad for:*** *wedding, grand opening*	*Rabbit*
Sat **2**	**Good for:** begin mission, school, planting ***Bad for:*** *funeral, lawsuit*	*Dragon*
Sun **3**	**Good for:** school, worship ***Bad for:*** *most activities*	*Snake*
Mon **4**	**Good for:** house cleaning ***Bad for:*** *begin mission, wedding, construction*	*Horse*
Tue **5**	**Good for:** worship, prayer ***Bad for:*** *most activities*	*Sheep*
Wed **6**	**Good for:** house cleaning ***Bad for:*** *wedding, grand opening, travel*	*Monkey*
Thu **7**	**Good for:** most activities ***Bad for:*** *burial, ground digging*	*Rooster*
Fri **8**	**Good for:** prayer, house cleaning ***Bad for:*** *most activities*	*Dog*
Sat **9**	**Good for:** worship, prayer ***Bad for:*** *begin mission, wedding, construction*	*Pig*
Sun **10**	⊖ **DON'T DO IMPORTANT THINGS** ⊖	*Rat*
Mon **11**	⊖ **DON'T DO IMPORTANT THINGS** ⊖	*Ox*
Tue **12**	**Good for:** contract, construction, buy property ***Bad for:*** *funeral, lawsuit*	*Tiger*
Wed **13**	**Good for:** most activities ***Bad for:*** *funeral, lawsuit*	*Rabbit*
Thu **14**	**Good for:** school, worship ***Bad for:*** *wedding, grand opening, travel*	*Dragon*
Fri **15**	**Good for:** worship, prayer ***Bad for:*** *most activities*	*Snake*

Sat **16**	**Good for:** worship, burial, ground digging *Bad for: lawsuit, surgery*	*Horse*
Sun **17**	**Good for:** contract, business, buy property *Bad for: burial, ground digging*	*Sheep*
Mon **18**	**Good for:** prayer, house cleaning *Bad for: wedding, grand opening, travel*	*Monkey*
Tue **19**	**Good for:** planting, worship *Bad for: contract, business*	*Rooster*
Wed **20**	**Good for:** school, worship *Bad for: begin mission, wedding, construction*	*Dog*
Thu **21**	**Good for:** most activities *Bad for: burial, funeral*	*Pig*
Fri **22**	**Good for:** grand opening, wedding, contract *Bad for: hunting, surgery*	*Rat*
Sat **23**	⊖ **DON'T DO IMPORTANT THINGS** ⊖	*Ox*
Sun **24**	**Good for:** worship, prayer *Bad for: most activities*	*Tiger*
Mon **25**	**Good for:** wedding, business, buy property *Bad for: ground digging, surgery*	*Rabbit*
Tue **26**	**Good for:** worship, prayer *Bad for: contract, business*	*Dragon*
Wed **27**	**Good for:** contract, business, buy property *Bad for: moving, travel, fix house*	*Snake*
Thu **28**	**Good for:** burial, worship, prayer *Bad for: moving, ground digging*	*Horse*
Fri **29**	**Good for:** worship, prayer *Bad for: most activities*	*Sheep*
Sat **30**	**Good for:** school, worship *Bad for: begin mission, wedding, construction*	*Monkey*
Sun **31**	**Good for:** prayer, house cleaning *Bad for: wedding, grand opening*	*Rooster*

February 2021

unfavorable for:

Mon **1**	**Good for:** burial, worship, prayer *Bad for: most activities*	*Dog*
Tue **2**	**Good for:** contract, business, buy property *Bad for: burial, funeral*	*Pig*
Wed **3**	⊖ **DON'T DO IMPORTANT THINGS** ⊖	*Rat*
Thu **4**	⊖ **DON'T DO IMPORTANT THINGS** ⊖	*Ox*
Fri **5**	**Good for:** prayer, house cleaning *Bad for: funeral, lawsuit*	*Tiger*
Sat **6**	**Good for:** prayer, planting *Bad for: wedding, contract*	*Rabbit*
Sun **7**	**Good for:** begin mission, contract *Bad for: ground digging, surgery*	*Dragon*
Mon **8**	**Good for:** most activities *Bad for: hunting, surgery*	*Snake*
Tue **9**	**Good for:** prayer, school, contract *Bad for: burial, grand opening*	*Horse*
Wed **10**	⊖ **DON'T DO IMPORTANT THINGS** ⊖	*Sheep*
Thu **11**	**Good for:** worship, prayer *Bad for: most activities*	*Monkey*
Fri **12**	**Good for:** wedding, grand opening, business *Bad for: burial, funeral*	*Rooster*
Sat **13**	**Good for:** most activities *Bad for: ground digging, surgery*	*Dog*
Sun **14**	**Good for:** worship, prayer *Bad for: wedding, grand opening*	*Pig*
Mon **15**	**Good for:** grand opening, wedding, contract *Bad for: ground digging, surgery*	*Rat*

Tue 16	⊖ **DON'T DO IMPORTANT THINGS** ⊖	Ox
Wed 17	⊖ **DON'T DO IMPORTANT THINGS** ⊖	Tiger
Thu 18	**Good for:** wedding, grand opening, business *Bad for: hunting, surgery*	Rabbit
Fri 19	**Good for:** worship, prayer *Bad for: grand opening, begin mission*	Dragon
Sat 20	**Good for:** most activities *Bad for: ground digging, surgery*	Snake
Sun 21	**Good for:** school, prayer, planting *Bad for: wedding, begin mission*	Horse
Mon 22	⊖ **DON'T DO IMPORTANT THINGS** ⊖	Sheep
Tue 23	**Good for:** grand opening, wedding, contract *Bad for: ground digging, surgery*	Monkey
Wed 24	**Good for:** contract, business, buy property *Bad for: funeral, lawsuit*	Rooster
Thu 25	**Good for:** worship, prayer *Bad for: most activities*	Dog
Fri 26	**Good for:** fix house, house cleaning *Bad for: business, begin mission*	Pig
Sat 27	**Good for:** wedding, contract, grand opening *Bad for: lawsuit, hunting*	Rat
Sun 28	⊖ **DON'T DO IMPORTANT THINGS** ⊖	Ox

S	M	T	W	T	F	S
	1	2	3	4	5	6
7	8	9	10	11	12	13
14	15	16	17	18	19	20
21	22	23	24	25	26	27
28	29	30	31			

March 2021

unfavorable for:

Mon **1**	⊖ **DON'T DO IMPORTANT THINGS** ⊖	*Tiger*
Tue **2**	**Good for:** worship, school, prayer *Bad for: grand opening, begin mission*	*Rabbit*
Wed **3**	**Good for:** house cleaning, planting *Bad for: wedding, grand opening*	*Dragon*
Thu **4**	**Good for:** wedding, business, buy property *Bad for: funeral, lawsuit*	*Snake*
Fri **5**	**Good for:** worship, prayer *Bad for: most activities*	*Horse*
Sat **6**	**Good for:** begin mission, school, planting *Bad for: wedding, contract*	*Sheep*
Sun **7**	**Good for:** contract, business, buy propery *Bad for: grand opening, surgery*	*Monkey*
Mon **8**	**Good for:** worship, prayer *Bad for: grand opening, begin mission*	*Rooster*
Tue **9**	**Good for:** contract, house cleaning, moving, prayer *Bad for: wedding, lawsuit, begin mission*	*Dog*
Wed **10**	**Good for:** wedding, business, buy property *Bad for: funeral, ground digging*	*Pig*
Thu **11**	**Good for:** worship, prayer *Bad for: most activities*	*Rat*
Fri **12**	⊖ **DON'T DO IMPORTANT THINGS** ⊖	*Ox*
Sat **13**	**Good for:** house cleaning, planting *Bad for: grand opening, begin mission*	*Tiger*
Sun **14**	⊖ **DON'T DO IMPORTANT THINGS** ⊖	*Rabbit*
Mon **15**	**Good for:** house cleaning, planting *Bad for: most activities*	*Dragon*

Tue 16	**Good for:** worship, prayer, planting *Bad for: grand opening, begin mission*	*Snake*
Wed 17	⊖ **DON'T DO IMPORTANT THINGS** ⊖	*Horse*
Thu 18	**Good for:** wedding, contract, grand opening *Bad for: ground digging, surgery*	*Sheep*
Fri 19	**Good for:** ground digging, contract, buy property *Bad for: lawsuit, hunting*	*Monkey*
Sat 20	**Good for:** most activities *Bad for: funeral, ground digging*	*Rooster*
Sun 21	**Good for:** begin mission, contract *Bad for: hunting, surgery*	*Dog*
Mon 22	**Good for:** grand opening, wedding, contract *Bad for: lawsuit, funeral*	*Pig*
Tue 23	**Good for:** worship, prayer *Bad for: most activities*	*Rat*
Wed 24	⊖ **DON'T DO IMPORTANT THINGS** ⊖	*Ox*
Thu 25	**Good for:** house cleaning, planting *Bad for: grand opening, begin mission*	*Tiger*
Fri 26	⊖ **DON'T DO IMPORTANT THINGS** ⊖	*Rabbit*
Sat 27	**Good for:** most activities *Bad for: lawsuit, hunting*	*Dragon*
Sun 28	**Good for:** begin mission, ground digging, school *Bad for: wedding, construction*	*Snake*
Mon 29	**Good for:** worship, prayer *Bad for: contract, buy property, wedding*	*Horse*
Tue 30	**Good for:** wedding, contract, grand opening *Bad for: ground digging, surgery*	*Sheep*
Wed 31	**Good for:** business, buy property, ground digging *Bad for: travel, moving*	*Monkey*

S	M	T	W	T	F	S
					1	2	3
4	5	6	7	8	9	10
11	12	13	14	15	16	17
18	19	20	21	22	23	24
25	26	27	28	29	30	

April 2021

unfavorable for:

Thu **1**	**Good for:** worship, prayer ***Bad for:*** *wedding, lawsuit, begin mission*	*Rooster*
Fri **2**	**Good for:** prayer, house cleaning ***Bad for:*** *most activities*	*Dog*
Sat **3**	**Good for:** grand opening, begin mission ***Bad for:*** *burial, funeral*	*Pig*
Sun **4**	**Good for:** most activities ***Bad for:*** *hunting, surgery*	*Rat*
Mon **5**	⚫ **DON'T DO IMPORTANT THINGS** ⚫	*Ox*
Tue **6**	**Good for:** worship, prayer ***Bad for:*** *wedding, construction*	*Tiger*
Wed **7**	**Good for:** wedding, contract, grand opening ***Bad for:*** *funeral, ground digging*	*Rabbit*
Thu **8**	**Good for:** worship, prayer ***Bad for:*** *most activities*	*Dragon*
Fri **9**	**Good for:** contract, construction, buy property ***Bad for:*** *hunting, surgery*	*Snake*
Sat **10**	**Good for:** most activities ***Bad for:*** *funeral, ground digging*	*Horse*
Sun **11**	**Good for:** prayer, house cleaning ***Bad for:*** *wedding, construction*	*Sheep*
Mon **12**	**Good for:** buy property, wedding, grand opening ***Bad for:*** *surgery, hunting, funeral*	*Monkey*
Tue **13**	**Good for:** fix house, house cleaning ***Bad for:*** *travel, moving*	*Rooster*
Wed **14**	**Good for:** worship, prayer ***Bad for:*** *surgery, wedding, begin mission*	*Dog*
Thu **15**	**Good for:** planting, house cleaning, school ***Bad for:*** *contract, buy property, wedding*	*Pig*

Fri **16**		**Good for:** worship, prayer, planting *Bad for: travel, moving, contract*	*Rat*
Sat **17**		⊖ **DON'T DO IMPORTANT THINGS** ⊖	*Ox*
Sun **18**		**Good for:** prayer, funeral, worship *Bad for: wedding, construction*	*Tiger*
Mon **19**		**Good for:** most activities *Bad for: hunting, surgery*	*Rabbit*
Tue **20**		⊖ **DON'T DO IMPORTANT THINGS** ⊖	*Dragon*
Wed **21**		**Good for:** school, planting *Bad for: contract, buy property*	*Snake*
Thu **22**		**Good for:** buy property, wedding, grand opening *Bad for: surgery, hunting, funeral*	*Horse*
Fri **23**		**Good for:** fix house, house cleaning *Bad for: travel, moving*	*Sheep*
Sat **24**		**Good for:** grand opening, wedding, contract *Bad for: hunting, surgery*	*Monkey*
Sun **25**		**Good for:** worship, prayer *Bad for: grand opening, wedding, contract*	*Rooster*
Mon **26**		**Good for:** school, planting, house cleaning *Bad for: ground digging, surgery*	*Dog*
Tue **27**		⊖ **DON'T DO IMPORTANT THINGS** ⊖	*Pig*
Wed **28**		**Good for:** worship, prayer *Bad for: wedding, construction*	*Rat*
Thu **29**		⊖ **DON'T DO IMPORTANT THINGS** ⊖	*Ox*
Fri **30**		**Good for:** prayer, house cleaning, funeral *Bad for: begin mission, wedding, construction*	*Tiger*

May 2021

S	M	T	W	T	F	S
						1
2	3	4	5	6	7	8
9	10	11	12	13	14	15
16	17	18	19	20	21	22
23	24	25	26	27	28	29
30	31					

unfavorable for:

Date		Unfavorable for
Sat 1	**Good for:** grand opening, wedding, contract ***Bad for:*** *surgery, lawsuit*	*Rabbit*
Sun 2	**Good for:** worship, prayer ***Bad for:*** *most activities*	*Dragon*
Mon 3	**Good for:** business, buy property, contract ***Bad for:*** *hunting, surgery*	*Snake*
Tue 4	⊖ **DON'T DO IMPORTANT THINGS** ⊖	*Horse*
Wed 5	**Good for:** grand opening, contract, buy property ***Bad for:*** *funeral, ground digging*	*Sheep*
Thu 6	**Good for:** fix house, house cleaning ***Bad for:*** *wedding, construction*	*Monkey*
Fri 7	**Good for:** most activities ***Bad for:*** *lawsuit, hunting*	*Rooster*
Sat 8	**Good for:** worship, prayer ***Bad for:*** *most activities*	*Dog*
Sun 9	**Good for:** school, planting, house cleaning ***Bad for:*** *wedding, construction*	*Pig*
Mon 10	**Good for:** worship, prayer ***Bad for:*** *most activities*	*Rat*
Tue 11	⊖ **DON'T DO IMPORTANT THINGS** ⊖	*Ox*
Wed 12	**Good for:** moving, wedding, grand opening ***Bad for:*** *lawsuit, hunting*	*Tiger*
Thu 13	**Good for:** most activities ***Bad for:*** *funeral, ground digging*	*Rabbit*
Fri 14	**Good for:** fix house, house cleaning ***Bad for:*** *wedding, construction*	*Dragon*
Sat 15	⊖ **DON'T DO IMPORTANT THINGS** ⊖	*Snake*

Sun 16	**Good for:** worship, prayer *Bad for: begin mission, wedding, construction*	*Horse*
Mon 17	**Good for:** grand opening, contract, buy property *Bad for: travel, moving*	*Sheep*
Tue 18	**Good for:** begin mission, wedding, construction *Bad for: lawsuit, hunting*	*Monkey*
Wed 19	**Good for:** worship, prayer *Bad for: wedding, construction*	*Rooster*
Thu 20	**Good for:** fix house, house cleaning *Bad for: most activities*	*Dog*
Fri 21	**Good for:** school, planting, house cleaning *Bad for: contract, business*	*Pig*
Sat 22	**Good for:** begin mission, wedding, construction *Bad for: burial, ground digging*	*Rat*
Sun 23	⊖ **DON'T DO IMPORTANT THINGS** ⊖	*Ox*
Mon 24	**Good for:** worship, prayer *Bad for: begin mission, wedding, construction*	*Tiger*
Tue 25	**Good for:** school, planting, house cleaning *Bad for: contract, business*	*Rabbit*
Wed 26	**Good for:** fix house, house cleaning *Bad for: wedding, construction*	*Dragon*
Thu 27	⊖ **DON'T DO IMPORTANT THINGS** ⊖	*Snake*
Fri 28	**Good for:** school, begin mission, prayer *Bad for: wedding, buy property*	*Horse*
Sat 29	**Good for:** grand opening, contract, buy propery *Bad for: burial, ground digging*	*Sheep*
Sun 30	**Good for:** worship, prayer *Bad for: begin mission, wedding, construction*	*Monkey*
Mon 31	**Good for:** fix house, house cleaning *Bad for: contract, business*	*Rooster*

S	M	T	W	T	F	S
		1	2	3	4	5
6	7	8	9	10	11	12
13	14	15	16	17	18	19
20	21	22	23	24	25	26
27	28	29	30			

June 2021

unfavorable for:

Tue **1**	**Good for:** planting, prayer, worship ***Bad for:*** *wedding, buy property*	*Dog*
Wed **2**	**Good for:** wedding, grand opening, business ***Bad for:*** *burial, ground digging*	*Pig*
Thu **3**	**Good for:** school, begin mission, prayer ***Bad for:*** *contract, business*	*Rat*
Fri **4**	⊖ **DON'T DO IMPORTANT THINGS** ⊖	*Ox*
Sat **5**	**Good for:** wedding, contract, grand opening ***Bad for:*** *funeral, lawsuit*	*Tiger*
Sun **6**	**Good for:** worship, prayer ***Bad for:*** *begin mission, wedding, construction*	*Rabbit*
Mon **7**	**Good for:** most activities ***Bad for:*** *burial, ground digging*	*Dragon*
Tue **8**	**Good for:** school, begin mission, prayer ***Bad for:*** *wedding, buy property*	*Snake*
Wed **9**	⊖ **DON'T DO IMPORTANT THINGS** ⊖	*Horse*
Thu **10**	**Good for:** fix house, house cleaning ***Bad for:*** *contract, business*	*Sheep*
Fri **11**	**Good for:** grand opening, contract, buy property ***Bad for:*** *funeral, lawsuit*	*Monkey*
Sat **12**	**Good for:** worship, prayer, planting ***Bad for:*** *wedding, buy property*	*Rooster*
Sun **13**	**Good for:** begin mission, contract, moving ***Bad for:*** *hunting, surgery*	*Dog*
Mon **14**	**Good for:** fix house, house cleaning ***Bad for:*** *contract, business*	*Pig*
Tue **15**	**Good for:** worship, prayer, planting ***Bad for:*** *wedding, buy property*	*Rat*

Wed 16	⊖ **DON'T DO IMPORTANT THINGS** ⊖	*Ox*
Thu 17	**Good for:** most activities *Bad for: hunting, surgery*	*Tiger*
Fri 18	**Good for:** worship, prayer, planting *Bad for: contract, business*	*Rabbit*
Sat 19	**Good for:** grand opening, contract, buy property *Bad for: lawsuit, ground digging*	*Dragon*
Sun 20	**Good for:** fix house, house cleaning *Bad for: grand opening, travel*	*Snake*
Mon 21	⊖ **DON'T DO IMPORTANT THINGS** ⊖	*Horse*
Tue 22	**Good for:** worship, prayer *Bad for: wedding, buy property*	*Sheep*
Wed 23	**Good for:** wedding, buy property, begin mission *Bad for: burial, funeral*	*Monkey*
Thu 24	**Good for:** worship, prayer *Bad for: wedding, grand opening*	*Rooster*
Fri 25	**Good for:** fix house, house cleaning *Bad for: contract, business*	*Dog*
Sat 26	**Good for:** worship, prayer, planting *Bad for: most activities*	*Pig*
Sun 27	**Good for:** prayer, planting *Bad for: lawsuit, contract*	*Rat*
Mon 28	⊖ **DON'T DO IMPORTANT THINGS** ⊖	*Ox*
Tue 29	**Good for:** grand opening, contract, buy property *Bad for: lawsuit, ground digging*	*Tiger*
Wed 30	**Good for:** worship, prayer *Bad for: wedding, grand opening*	*Rabbit*

S	M	T	W	T	F	S
				1	2	3
4	5	6	7	8	9	10
11	12	13	14	15	16	17
18	19	20	21	22	23	24
25	26	27	28	29	30	31

July 2021

unfavorable for:

Day		Unfavorable
Thu **1**	**Good for:** wedding, buy property, begin mission *Bad for:* burial, funeral	*Dragon*
Fri **2**	**Good for:** fix house, house cleaning *Bad for:* contract, business	*Snake*
Sat **3**	⊖ **DON'T DO IMPORTANT THINGS** ⊖	*Horse*
Sun **4**	**Good for:** prayer, planting *Bad for:* wedding, grand opening, travel	*Sheep*
Mon **5**	**Good for:** most activities *Bad for:* lawsuit, ground digging	*Monkey*
Tue **6**	**Good for:** worship, prayer, planting *Bad for:* wedding, grand opening	*Rooster*
Wed **7**	**Good for:** fix house, house cleaning *Bad for:* contract, business	*Dog*
Thu **8**	**Good for:** prayer, planting *Bad for:* travel, buy property, construction	*Pig*
Fri **9**	**Good for:** worship, house cleaning *Bad for:* wedding, grand opening	*Rat*
Sat **10**	⊖ **DON'T DO IMPORTANT THINGS** ⊖	*Ox*
Sun **11**	**Good for:** worship, prayer, planting *Bad for:* contract, business	*Tiger*
Mon **12**	**Good for:** house cleaning, planting *Bad for:* wedding, grand opening	*Rabbit*
Tue **13**	⊖ **DON'T DO IMPORTANT THINGS** ⊖	*Dragon*
Wed **14**	**Good for:** worship, prayer, planting *Bad for:* travel, buy property, construction	*Snake*
Thu **15**	**Good for:** wedding, buy property, begin mission *Bad for:* burial, funeral	*Horse*

Fri 16	**Good for:** prayer, planting ***Bad for:*** *contract, business*	*Sheep*
Sat 17	**Good for:** most activities ***Bad for:*** *lawsuit, surgery*	*Monkey*
Sun 18	**Good for:** contract, construction, buy property ***Bad for:*** *ground digging, surgery*	*Rooster*
Mon 19	**Good for:** house cleaning, planting ***Bad for:*** *worship, school*	*Dog*
Tue 20	**Good for:** begin mission, school, planting ***Bad for:*** *lawsuit, contract*	*Pig*
Wed 21	**Good for:** fix house, house cleaning ***Bad for:*** *contract, business, buy property*	*Rat*
Thu 22	⊖ **DON'T DO IMPORTANT THINGS** ⊖	*Ox*
Fri 23	**Good for:** school, worship ***Bad for:*** *travel, buy property, construction*	*Tiger*
Sat 24	**Good for:** prayer, planting ***Bad for:*** *wedding, grand opening*	*Rabbit*
Sun 25	**Good for:** fix house, house cleaning ***Bad for:*** *ground digging, surgery*	*Dragon*
Mon 26	**Good for:** business, begin mission, contract ***Bad for:*** *lawsuit, ground digging*	*Snake*
Tue 27	**Good for:** prayer, house cleaning ***Bad for:*** *grand opening, begin mission*	*Horse*
Wed 28	⊖ **DON'T DO IMPORTANT THINGS** ⊖	*Sheep*
Thu 29	**Good for:** business, begin mission, contract ***Bad for:*** *lawsuit, ground digging*	*Monkey*
Fri 30	**Good for:** wedding, contract, grand opening ***Bad for:*** *funeral, lawsuit*	*Rooster*
Sat 31	**Good for:** prayer, planting ***Bad for:*** *wedding, grand opening*	*Dog*

S	M	T	W	T	F	S
1	2	3	4	5	6	7
8	9	10	11	12	13	14
15	16	17	18	19	20	21
22	23	24	25	26	27	28
29	30	31				

August 2021

unfavorable for:

Sun **1**	**Good for:** begin mission, school, planting ***Bad for:*** *funeral, lawsuit*	*Pig*
Mon **2**	**Good for:** prayer, house cleaning ***Bad for:*** *ground digging, surgery*	*Rat*
Tue **3**	⊖ **DON'T DO IMPORTANT THINGS** ⊖	*Ox*
Wed **4**	**Good for:** begin mission, contract, planting ***Bad for:*** *lawsuit, surgery*	*Tiger*
Thu **5**	**Good for:** ground digging, funeral, prayer ***Bad for:*** *wedding, grand opening*	*Rabbit*
Fri **6**	**Good for:** prayer, planting ***Bad for:*** *lawsuit, ground digging*	*Dragon*
Sat **7**	**Good for:** business, begin mission, contract ***Bad for:*** *funeral, lawsuit*	*Snake*
Sun **8**	**Good for:** wedding, grand opening, begin mission ***Bad for:*** *hunting, surgery*	*Horse*
Mon **9**	**Good for:** prayer, planting ***Bad for:*** *wedding, grand opening*	*Sheep*
Tue **10**	⊖ **DON'T DO IMPORTANT THINGS** ⊖	*Monkey*
Wed **11**	**Good for:** prayer, house cleaning ***Bad for:*** *business, begin mission, contract*	*Rooster*
Thu **12**	**Good for:** contract, business, buy property ***Bad for:*** *ground digging, surgery*	*Dog*
Fri **13**	**Good for:** most activities ***Bad for:*** *funeral, lawsuit*	*Pig*
Sat **14**	**Good for:** begin mission, contract, planting ***Bad for:*** *hunting, surgery*	*Rat*
Sun **15**	⊖ **DON'T DO IMPORTANT THINGS** ⊖	*Ox*

Mon **16**	**Good for:** prayer, house cleaning *Bad for: wedding, contract*	*Tiger*
Tue **17**	**Good for:** ground digging, funeral, prayer *Bad for: business, begin mission, contract*	*Rabbit*
Wed **18**	**Good for:** wedding, contract, grand opening *Bad for: burial, funeral*	*Dragon*
Thu **19**	**Good for:** worship, prayer *Bad for: contract, business*	*Snake*
Fri **20**	**Good for:** most activities *Bad for: funeral, lawsuit*	*Horse*
Sat **21**	**Good for:** school, worship *Bad for: ground digging, surgery*	*Sheep*
Sun **22**	⚊ **DON'T DO IMPORTANT THINGS** ⚊	*Monkey*
Mon **23**	**Good for:** wedding, buy property, begin mission *Bad for: hunting, surgery*	*Rooster*
Tue **24**	**Good for:** prayer, house cleaning *Bad for: wedding, grand opening*	*Dog*
Wed **25**	**Good for:** worship, prayer *Bad for: wedding, travel*	*Pig*
Thu **26**	**Good for:** school, worship *Bad for: most activities*	*Rat*
Fri **27**	⚊ **DON'T DO IMPORTANT THINGS** ⚊	*Ox*
Sat **28**	**Good for:** wedding, contract, grand opening *Bad for: burial, funeral*	*Tiger*
Sun **29**	**Good for:** ground digging, burial *Bad for: wedding, travel*	*Rabbit*
Mon **30**	**Good for:** prayer, planting *Bad for: contract, buy property*	*Dragon*
Tues **31**	**Good for:** fix house, house cleaning *Bad for: contract, business*	*Snake*

S	M	T	W	T	F	S
			1	2	3	4
5	6	7	8	9	10	11
12	13	14	15	16	17	18
19	20	21	22	23	24	25
26	27	28	29	30		

September 2021

unfavorable for:

Wed **1**	**Good for:** most activities *Bad for: hunting, surgery*	*Horse*
Thu **2**	**Good for:** business, begin mission, contract *Bad for: burial, funeral*	*Sheep*
Fri **3**	⊖ **DON'T DO IMPORTANT THINGS** ⊖	*Monkey*
Sat **4**	⊖ **DON'T DO IMPORTANT THINGS** ⊖	*Rooster*
Sun **5**	**Good for:** school, begin mission, prayer *Bad for: contract, buy property*	*Dog*
Mon **6**	**Good for:** wedding, contract, grand opening *Bad for: hunting, surgery*	*Pig*
Tue **7**	**Good for:** prayer, planting *Bad for: contract, buy property*	*Rat*
Wed **8**	⊖ **DON'T DO IMPORTANT THINGS** ⊖	*Ox*
Thu **9**	**Good for:** business, begin mission, contract *Bad for: burial, funeral*	*Tiger*
Fri **10**	**Good for:** school, begin mission, prayer *Bad for: wedding, travel*	*Rabbit*
Sat **11**	**Good for:** contract, business, buy property *Bad for: moving, travel, fix house*	*Dragon*
Sun **12**	⊖ **DON'T DO IMPORTANT THINGS** ⊖	*Snake*
Mon **13**	**Good for:** fix house, house cleaning *Bad for: contract, business*	*Horse*
Tue **14**	**Good for:** wedding, contract, grand opening *Bad for: hunting, surgery*	*Sheep*
Wed **15**	**Good for:** prayer, planting *Bad for: contract, buy property*	*Monkey*

Thu **16**	⊖ DON'T DO IMPORTANT THINGS ⊖	Rooster
Fri **17**	**Good for:** worship, prayer *Bad for: contract, business*	Dog
Sat **18**	**Good for:** moving, wedding, grand opening *Bad for: hunting, surgery*	Pig
Sun **19**	**Good for:** business, begin mission, contract *Bad for: moving, travel, fix house*	Rat
Mon **20**	⊖ DON'T DO IMPORTANT THINGS ⊖	Ox
Tue **21**	**Good for:** begin mission, contract, planting *Bad for: wedding, grand opening*	Tiger
Wed **22**	**Good for:** worship, prayer *Bad for: contract, buy property*	Rabbit
Thu **23**	**Good for:** begin mission, school, planting *Bad for: funeral, lawsuit*	Dragon
Fri **24**	**Good for:** wedding, grand opening, contract *Bad for: burial, ground digging*	Snake
Sat **25**	**Good for:** worship, prayer *Bad for: contract, business*	Horse
Sun **26**	**Good for:** begin mission, wedding, construction *Bad for: burial, funeral*	Sheep
Mon **27**	⊖ DON'T DO IMPORTANT THINGS ⊖	Monkey
Tue **28**	⊖ DON'T DO IMPORTANT THINGS ⊖	Rooster
Wed **29**	**Good for:** most activities *Bad for: burial, ground digging*	Dog
Thu **30**	**Good for:** wedding, contract, grand opening *Bad for: funeral, lawsuit*	Pig

October 2021

unfavorable for:

Day		Zodiac
Fri **1**	**Good for:** school, worship *Bad for: wedding, grand opening, travel*	*Rat*
Sat **2**	⛔ **DON'T DO IMPORTANT THINGS** ⛔	*Ox*
Sun **3**	**Good for:** begin mission, contract, planting *Bad for: funeral, lawsuit*	*Tiger*
Mon **4**	**Good for:** fix house, house cleaning *Bad for: contract, business*	*Rabbit*
Tue **5**	**Good for:** begin mission, school, planting *Bad for: burial, funeral*	*Dragon*
Wed **6**	**Good for:** school, worship *Bad for: burial, ground digging*	*Snake*
Thu **7**	**Good for:** prayer, house cleaning *Bad for: wedding, grand opening*	*Horse*
Fri **8**	⛔ **DON'T DO IMPORTANT THINGS** ⛔	*Sheep*
Sat **9**	**Good for:** fix house, house cleaning *Bad for: burial, ground digging*	*Monkey*
Sun **10**	**Good for:** wedding, buy property, begin misson *Bad for: hunting, surgery*	*Rooster*
Mon **11**	⛔ **DON'T DO IMPORTANT THINGS** ⛔	*Dog*
Tue **12**	**Good for:** business, begin mission, contract *Bad for: lawsuit, ground digging*	*Pig*
Wed **13**	**Good for:** wedding, buy property, begin mission *Bad for: ground digging, surgery*	*Rat*
Thu **14**	⛔ **DON'T DO IMPORTANT THINGS** ⛔	*Ox*
Fri **15**	**Good for:** begin mission, wedding, construction *Bad for: funeral, lawsuit*	*Tiger*

Sat **16**	**Good for:** prayer, house cleaning *Bad for:* burial, ground digging	*Rabbit*
Sun **17**	**Good for:** worship, prayer *Bad for:* wedding, grand opening	*Dragon*
Mon **18**	**Good for:** prayer, planting *Bad for:* contract, business, buy property	*Snake*
Tue **19**	**Good for:** fix house, house cleaning *Bad for:* lawsuit, ground digging	*Horse*
Wed **20**	**Good for:** school, worship *Bad for:* wedding, grand opening, travel	*Sheep*
Thu **21**	**Good for:** school, house cleaning *Bad for:* contract, grand opening	*Monkey*
Fri **22**	**Good for:** most activities *Bad for:* lawsuit, travel, surgery	*Rooster*
Sat **23**	⊖ **DON'T DO IMPORTANT THINGS** ⊖	*Dog*
Sun **24**	**Good for:** prayer, house cleaning *Bad for:* contract, business, buy property	*Pig*
Mon **25**	**Good for:** wedding, grand opening, begin mission *Bad for:* funeral, lawsuit	*Rat*
Tue **26**	⊖ **DON'T DO IMPORTANT THINGS** ⊖	*Ox*
Wed **27**	**Good for:** most activities *Bad for:* hunting, surgery	*Tiger*
Thu **28**	**Good for:** fix house, planting *Bad for:* wedding, grand opening, travel	*Rabbit*
Fri **29**	**Good for:** worship, prayer *Bad for:* most activities	*Dragon*
Sat **30**	**Good for:** business, begin mission, contract *Bad for:* lawsuit, ground digging	*Snake*
Sun **31**	**Good for:** prayer, house cleaning *Bad for:* contract, grand opening	*Horse*

S	M	T	W	T	F	S
	1	2	3	4	5	6
7	8	9	10	11	12	13
14	15	16	17	18	19	20
21	22	23	24	25	26	27
28	29	30				

November 2021

unfavorable for:

Mon **1**	**Good for:** fix house, planting *Bad for:* contract, business, buy property	*Sheep*
Tue **2**	**Good for:** school, planting *Bad for:* surgery, lawsuit	*Monkey*
Wed **3**	**Good for:** school, worship *Bad for:* burial, ground digging	*Rooster*
Thu **4**	⬤ **DON'T DO IMPORTANT THINGS** ⬤	*Dog*
Fri **5**	**Good for:** planting, house cleaning, worship *Bad for:* wedding, begin mission, surgery	*Pig*
Sat **6**	**Good for:** grand opening, contract, buy property *Bad for:* ground digging, surgery	*Rat*
Sun **7**	⬤ **DON'T DO IMPORTANT THINGS** ⬤	*Ox*
Mon **8**	**Good for:** begin mission, construction, fix house *Bad for:* funeral, lawsuit	*Tiger*
Tue **9**	**Good for:** begin mission, school, planting *Bad for:* lawsuit, travel, surgery	*Rabbit*
Wed **10**	**Good for:** prayer, house cleaning *Bad for:* contract, grand opening	*Dragon*
Thu **11**	⬤ **DON'T DO IMPORTANT THINGS** ⬤	*Snake*
Fri **12**	**Good for:** most activities *Bad for:* ground digging, surgery	*Horse*
Sat **13**	**Good for:** worship, prayer *Bad for:* wedding, begin mission, surgery	*Sheep*
Sun **14**	**Good for:** wedding, grand opening, business *Bad for:* funeral, lawsuit	*Monkey*
Mon **15**	**Good for:** begin mission, wedding, construction *Bad for:* surgery, lawsuit	*Rooster*

Tue **16**	**Good for:** worship, prayer ***Bad for:*** *ground digging, surgery*	*Dog*
Wed **17**	⊖ **DON'T DO IMPORTANT THINGS** ⊖	*Pig*
Thu **18**	**Good for:** fix house, planting ***Bad for:*** *contract, grand opening*	*Rat*
Fri **19**	⊖ **DON'T DO IMPORTANT THINGS** ⊖	*Ox*
Sat **20**	**Good for:** prayer, house cleaning ***Bad for:*** *grand opening, begin mission*	*Tiger*
Sun **21**	**Good for:** school, worship ***Bad for:*** *wedding, grand opening, travel*	*Rabbit*
Mon **22**	**Good for:** worship, prayer ***Bad for:*** *begin mission, surgery*	*Dragon*
Tue **23**	**Good for:** planting, house cleaning, worship ***Bad for:*** *contract, business*	*Snake*
Wed **24**	**Good for:** begin mission, construction, fix house ***Bad for:*** *funeral, lawsuit*	*Horse*
Thu **25**	**Good for:** prayer, house cleaning ***Bad for:*** *wedding, grand opening, contract*	*Sheep*
Fri **26**	**Good for:** grand opening, begin mission ***Bad for:*** *hunting, surgery*	*Monkey*
Sat **27**	**Good for:** wedding, buy property, business ***Bad for:*** *funeral, lawsuit*	*Rooster*
Sun **28**	**Good for:** moving, wedding, grand opening ***Bad for:*** *ground digging, surgery*	*Dog*
Mon **29**	⊖ **DON'T DO IMPORTANT THINGS** ⊖	*Pig*
Tue **30**	**Good for:** prayer, house cleaning ***Bad for:*** *grand opening, begin mission*	*Rat*

S	M	T	W	T	F	S
			1	2	3	4
5	6	7	8	9	10	11
12	13	14	15	16	17	18
19	20	21	22	23	24	25
26	27	28	29	30	31	

December 2021

unfavorable for:

Day		Unfavorable
Wed 1	⊖ **DON'T DO IMPORTANT THINGS** ⊖	*Ox*
Thu 2	**Good for:** planting, house cleaning, worship ***Bad for:*** *contract, business, grand opening*	*Tiger*
Fri 3	**Good for:** wedding, grand opening, business ***Bad for:*** *ground digging, surgery*	*Rabbit*
Sat 4	**Good for:** planting, house cleaning, worship ***Bad for:*** *begin mission, surgery*	*Dragon*
Sun 5	**Good for:** school, worship ***Bad for:*** *contract, business*	*Snake*
Mon 6	⊖ **DON'T DO IMPORTANT THINGS** ⊖	*Horse*
Tue 7	**Good for:** prayer, house cleaning ***Bad for:*** *ground digging, surgery*	*Sheep*
Wed 8	**Good for:** contract, begin mission, wedding ***Bad for:*** *funeral, lawsuit*	*Monkey*
Thu 9	**Good for:** worship, prayer ***Bad for:*** *grand opening, begin mission*	*Rooster*
Fri 10	**Good for:** most activities ***Bad for:*** *ground digging, surgery*	*Dog*
Sat 11	**Good for:** funeral, burial, worship ***Bad for:*** *contract, business*	*Pig*
Sun 12	⊖ **DON'T DO IMPORTANT THINGS** ⊖	*Rat*
Mon 13	⊖ **DON'T DO IMPORTANT THINGS** ⊖	*Ox*
Tue 14	**Good for:** worship, prayer ***Bad for:*** *contract, buy property*	*Tiger*
Wed 15	**Good for:** school, house cleaning ***Bad for:*** *moving, travel*	*Rabbit*

Thu **16**	**Good for:** prayer, planting *Bad for: lawsuit, contract*	*Dragon*
Fri **17**	**Good for:** funeral, burial, worship *Bad for: begin mission, surgery*	*Snake*
Sat **18**	⊖ **DON'T DO IMPORTANT THINGS** ⊖	*Horse*
Sun **19**	**Good for:** business, begin mission, contract *Bad for: ground digging, surgery*	*Sheep*
Mon **20**	**Good for:** most activities *Bad for: funeral, lawsuit*	*Monkey*
Tue **21**	**Good for:** planting, house cleaning, worship *Bad for: contract, business, grand opening*	*Rooster*
Wed **22**	**Good for:** begin mission, wedding, contruction *Bad for: lawsuit, ground digging*	*Dog*
Thu **23**	**Good for:** burial, ground digging *Bad for: buy property, begin mission*	*Pig*
Fri **24**	⊖ **DON'T DO IMPORTANT THINGS** ⊖	*Rat*
Sat **25**	⊖ **DON'T DO IMPORTANT THINGS** ⊖	*Ox*
Sun **26**	**Good for:** wedding, contract, grand opening *Bad for: funeral, lawsuit*	*Tiger*
Mon **27**	**Good for:** school, worship *Bad for: contract, business, grand opening*	*Rabbit*
Tue **28**	**Good for:** contract, business, buy property *Bad for: burial, ground digging*	*Dragon*
Wed **29**	**Good for:** prayer, planting *Bad for: lawsuit, contract*	*Snake*
Thu **30**	⊖ **DON'T DO IMPORTANT THINGS** ⊖	*Horse*
Fri **31**	**Good for:** moving, wedding, grand opening *Bad for: burial, ground digging*	*Sheep*

S	M	T	W	T	F	S
						1
2	3	4	5	6	7	8
9	10	11	12	13	14	15
16	17	18	19	20	21	22
23	24	25	26	27	28	29
30	31					

January 2022

unfavorable for:

Sat **1**	**Good for:** begin mission, construction, fix house ***Bad for:*** *lawsuit, travel, surgery*	*Monkey*
Sun **2**	**Good for:** funeral, burial, worship ***Bad for:*** *buy property, begin mission*	*Rooster*
Mon **3**	**Good for:** wedding, buy property, begin mission ***Bad for:*** *burial, funeral*	*Dog*
Tue **4**	**Good for:** worship, prayer ***Bad for:*** *most activities*	*Pig*
Wed **5**	⊖ **DON'T DO IMPORTANT THINGS** ⊖	*Rat*
Thu **6**	⊖ **DON'T DO IMPORTANT THINGS** ⊖	*Ox*
Fri **7**	**Good for:** wedding, contract, grand opening ***Bad for:*** *hunting, surgery*	*Tiger*
Sat **8**	**Good for:** most activities ***Bad for:*** *burial, ground digging*	*Rabbit*
Sun **9**	**Good for:** prayer, planting ***Bad for:*** *lawsuit, contract*	*Dragon*
Mon **10**	**Good for:** fix house, house cleaning ***Bad for:*** *contract, buy property*	*Snake*
Tue **11**	**Good for:** burial, ground digging ***Bad for:*** *wedding, grand opening, contract*	*Horse*
Wed **12**	**Good for:** wedding, grand opening, begin mission ***Bad for:*** *burial, ground digging*	*Sheep*
Thu **13**	⊖ **DON'T DO IMPORTANT THINGS** ⊖	*Monkey*
Fri **14**	**Good for:** worship, prayer ***Bad for:*** *buy property, begin mission*	*Rooster*
Sat **15**	**Good for:** house cleaning, worship ***Bad for:*** *contract, buy property*	*Dog*

Sun **16**	**Good for:** wedding, grand opening, contract *Bad for: burial, ground digging*	*Pig*
Mon **17**	⊖ **DON'T DO IMPORTANT THINGS** ⊖	*Rat*
Tue **18**	⊖ **DON'T DO IMPORTANT THINGS** ⊖	*Ox*
Wed **19**	**Good for:** school, house cleaning *Bad for: wedding, grand opening, contract*	*Tiger*
Thu **20**	**Good for:** wedding, buy property, begin mission *Bad for: funeral, lawsuit*	*Rabbit*
Fri **21**	**Good for:** fix house, planting *Bad for: contract, business*	*Dragon*
Sat **22**	**Good for:** begin mission, school, planting *Bad for: contract, buy property*	*Snake*
Sun **23**	**Good for:** worship, prayer *Bad for: begin mission, construction*	*Horse*
Mon **24**	⊖ **DON'T DO IMPORTANT THINGS** ⊖	*Sheep*
Tue **25**	**Good for:** house cleaning, worship *Bad for: burial, ground digging*	*Monkey*
Wed **26**	**Good for:** worship, prayer *Bad for: begin mission, contract*	*Rooster*
Thu **27**	**Good for:** planting, house cleaning, worship *Bad for: wedding, grand opening, contract*	*Dog*
Fri **28**	**Good for:** begin mission, contract, business *Bad for: funeral, lawsuit*	*Pig*
Sat **29**	⊖ **DON'T DO IMPORTANT THINGS** ⊖	*Rat*
Sun **30**	⊖ **DON'T DO IMPORTANT THINGS** ⊖	*Ox*
Mon **31**	**Good for:** grand opening, contract, buy property *Bad for: hunting, surgery*	*Tiger*

前事不忘
後事之師

Calligraphy by Larry Sang

When you lose,
don't lose the lesson.

TEN THOUSAND YEAR CALENDAR

TEN-THOUSAND YEAR CALENDAR

	1ST MONTH Gen Yin	2ND MONTH Xin Mao	3RD MONTH Ren Chen	4TH MONTH Gui Si	5TH MONTH Jia Wu	6TH MONTH Yi Wei	
1	2/12 Xin Mao	3/13 Geng Shen	4/12 Geng Yin	5/12 Geng Shen	6/10 Ji Chou	7/10 Ji Wei	1
2	2/13 Ren Chen	3/14 Xin You	4/13 Xin Mao	5/13 Xin You	6/11 Geng Yin	7/11 Geng Shen	2
3	2/14 Gui Si	3/15 Ren Xu	4/14 Ren Chen	5/14 Ren Xu	6/12 Xin Mao	7/12 Xin You	3
4	2/15 Jia Wu	3/16 Gui Hai	4/15 Gui Si	5/15 Gui Hai	6/13 Ren Chen	7/13 Ren Xu	4
5	2/16 Yi Wei	3/17 Jia Zi	4/16 Jia Wu	5/16 Jia Zi	6/14 Gui Si	7/14 Gui Hai	5
6	2/17 Bing Shen	3/18 Yi Chou	4/17 Yi Wei	5/17 Yi Chou	6/15 Jia Wu	7/15 Jia Zi	6
7	2/18 Ding You	3/19 Bing Yin	4/18 Bing Shen	5/18 Bing Yin	6/16 Yi Wei	7/16 Yi Chou	7
8	2/19 Wu Xu	3/20 Ding Mao	4/19 Ding You	5/19 Ding Mao	6/17 Bing Shen	7/17 Bing Yin	8
9	2/20 Ji Hai	3/21 Wu Chen	4/20 Wu Xu	5/20 Wu Chen	6/18 Ding You	7/18 Ding Mao	9
10	2/21 Geng Zi	3/22 Ji Si	4/21 Ji Hai	5/21 Ji Si	6/19 Wu Xu	7/19 Wu Chen	10
11	2/22 Xin Chou	3/23 Geng Wu	4/22 Geng Zi	5/22 Geng Wu	6/20 Ji Hai	7/20 Ji Si	11
12	2/23 Ren Yin	3/24 Xin Wei	4/23 Xin Chou	5/23 Xin Wei	6/21 Geng Zi	7/21 Geng Wu	12
13	2/24 Gui Mao	3/25 Ren Shen	4/24 Ren Yin	5/24 Ren Shen	6/22 Xin Chou	7/22 Xin Wei	13
14	2/25 Jia Chen	3/26 Gui You	4/25 Gui Mao	5/25 Gui You	6/23 Ren Yin	7/23 Ren Shen	14
15	2/26 Yi Si	3/27 Jia Xu	4/26 Jia Chen	5/26 Jia Xu	6/24 Gui Mao	7/24 Gui You	15
16	2/27 Bing Wu	3/28 Yi Hai	4/27 Yi Si	5/27 Yi Hai	6/25 Jia Chen	7/25 Jia Xu	16
17	2/28 Ding Wei	3/29 Bing Zi	4/28 Bing Wu	5/28 Bing Zi	6/26 Yi Si	7/26 Yi Hai	17
18	3/1 Wu Shen	3/30 Ding Chou	4/29 Ding Wei	5/29 Ding Chou	6/27 Bing Wu	7/27 Bing Zi	18
19	3/2 Ji You	3/31 Wu Yin	4/30 Wu Shen	5/30 Wu Yin	6/28 Ding Wei	7/28 Ding Chou	19
20	3/3 Geng Xu	4/1 Ji Mao	5/1 Ji You	5/31 Ji Mao	6/29 Wu Shen	7/29 Wu Yin	20
21	3/4 Xin Hai	4/2 Geng Chen	5/2 Geng Xu	6/1 Geng Chen	6/30 Ji You	7/30 Ji Mao	21
22	3/5 Ren Zi	4/3 Xin Si	5/3 Xin Hai	6/2 Xin Si	7/1 Geng Xu	7/31 Geng Chen	22
23	3/6 Gui Chou	4/4 Ren Wu	5/4 Ren Zi	6/3 Ren Wu	7/2 Xin Hai	8/1 Xin Si	23
24	3/7 Jia Yin	4/5 Gui Wei	5/5 Gui Chou	6/4 Gui Wei	7/3 Ren Zi	8/2 Ren Wu	24
25	3/8 Yi Mao	4/6 Jia Shen	5/6 Jia Yin	6/5 Jia Shen	7/4 Gui Chou	8/3 Gui Wei	25
26	3/9 Bing Chen	4/7 Yi You	5/7 Yi Mao	6/6 Yi You	7/5 Jia Yin	8/4 Jia Shen	26
27	3/10 Ding Si	4/8 Bing Xu	5/8 Bing Chen	6/7 Bing Xu	7/6 Yi Mao	8/5 Yi You	27
28	3/11 Wu Wu	4/9 Ding Hai	5/9 Ding Si	6/8 Ding Hai	7/7 Bing Chen	8/6 Bing Xu	28
29	3/12 Ji Wei	4/10 Wu Zi	5/10 Wu Wu	6/9 Wu Zi	7/8 Ding Si	8/7 Ding Hai	29
30		4/11 Ji Chou	5/11 Ji Wei		7/9 Wu Wu		30
	5 Yellow	**4 Green**	**3 Jade**	**2 Black**	**1 White**	**9 Purple**	
Jie	**Li Chun** 2/3 11:08pm	**Jing Zhi** 3/5 4:54pm	**Qing Ming** 4/4 9:37pm	**Li Xia** 5/5 2:57pm	**Mang Zhong** 6/5 7:09pm	**Xiao Shu** 7/7 5:33am	**Jie**
Qi	**Yu Shui** 2/18 6:51pm	**Chun Fen** 3/20 5:42pm	**Gu Yu** 4/20 4:44am	**Xiao Man** 5/21 3:56am	**Xia Zhi** 6/21 11:58am	**Da Shu** 7/22 11:05pm	**Qi**

Year: Xin Chou • 6 White   **2021**

	7TH MONTH Bing Shen		8TH MONTH Ding You		9TH MONTH Wu Xu		10TH MONTH Ji Hai		11TH MONTH Gen Zi		12TH MONTH Xin Chou	
									2021-2022				
1	8/8	Wu Zi	9/7	Wu Wu	10/6	Ding Hai	11/5	Ding Si	12/4	Bing Xu	1/3	Bing Chen	1
2	8/9	Ji Chou	9/8	Ji Wei	10/7	Wu Zi	11/6	Wu Wu	12/5	Ding Hai	1/4	Ding Si	2
3	8/10	Geng Yin	9/9	Geng Shen	10/8	Ji Chou	11/7	Ji Wei	12/6	Wu Zi	1/5	Wu Wu	3
4	8/11	Xin Mao	9/10	Xin You	10/9	Geng Yin	11/8	Geng Shen	12/7	Ji Chou	1/6	Ji Wei	4
5	8/12	Ren Chen	9/11	Ren Xu	10/10	Xin Mao	11/9	Xin You	12/8	Geng Yin	1/7	Geng Shen	5
6	8/13	Gui Si	9/12	Gui Hai	10/11	Ren Chen	11/10	Ren Xu	12/9	Xin Mao	1/8	Xin You	6
7	8/14	Jia Wu	9/13	Jia Zi	10/12	Gui Si	11/11	Gui Hai	12/10	Ren Chen	1/9	Ren Xu	7
8	8/15	Yi Wei	9/14	Yi Chou	10/13	Jia Wu	11/12	Jia Zi	12/11	Gui Si	1/10	Gui Hai	8
9	8/16	Bing Shen	9/15	Bing Yin	10/14	Yi Wei	11/13	Yi Chou	12/12	Jia Wu	1/11	Jia Zi	9
10	8/17	Ding You	9/16	Ding Mao	10/15	Bing Shen	11/14	Bing Yin	12/13	Yi Wei	1/12	Yi Chou	10
11	8/18	Wu Xu	9/17	Wu Chen	10/16	Ding You	11/15	Ding Mao	12/14	Bing Shen	1/13	Bing Yin	11
12	8/19	Ji Hai	9/18	Ji Si	10/17	Wu Xu	11/16	Wu Chen	12/15	Ding You	1/14	Ding Mao	12
13	8/20	Geng Zi	9/19	Geng Wu	10/18	Ji Hai	11/17	Ji Si	12/16	Wu Xu	1/15	Wu Chen	13
14	8/21	Xin Chou	9/20	Xin Wei	10/19	Geng Zi	11/18	Geng Wu	12/17	Ji Hai	1/16	Ji Si	14
15	8/22	Ren Yin	9/21	Ren Shen	10/20	Xin Chou	11/19	Xin Wei	12/18	Geng Zi	1/17	Geng Wu	15
16	8/23	Gui Mao	9/22	Gui You	10/21	Ren Yin	11/20	Ren Shen	12/19	Xin Chou	1/18	Xin Wei	16
17	8/24	Jia Chen	9/23	Jia Xu	10/22	Gui Mao	11/21	Gui You	12/20	Ren Yin	1/19	Ren Shen	17
18	8/25	Yi Si	9/24	Yi Hai	10/23	Jia Chen	11/22	Jia Xu	12/21	Gui Mao	1/20	Gui You	18
19	8/26	Bing Wu	9/25	Bing Zi	10/24	Yi Si	11/23	Yi Hai	12/22	Jia Chen	1/21	Jia Xu	19
20	8/27	Ding Wei	9/26	Ding Chou	10/25	Bing Wu	11/24	Bing Zi	12/23	Yi Si	1/22	Yi Hai	20
21	8/28	Wu Shen	9/27	Wu Yin	10/26	Ding Wei	11/25	Ding Chou	12/24	Bing Wu	1/23	Bing Zi	21
22	8/29	Ji You	9/28	Ji Mao	10/27	Wu Shen	11/26	Wu Yin	12/25	Ding Wei	1/24	Ding Chou	22
23	8/30	Geng Xu	9/29	Geng Chen	10/28	Ji You	11/27	Ji Mao	12/26	Wu Shen	1/25	Wu Yin	23
24	8/31	Xin Hai	9/30	Xin Si	10/29	Geng Xu	11/28	Geng Chen	12/27	Ji You	1/26	Ji Mao	24
25	9/1	Ren Zi	10/1	Ren Wu	10/30	Xin Hai	11/29	Xin Si	12/28	Geng Xu	1/27	Geng Chen	25
26	9/2	Gui Chou	10/2	Gui Wei	10/31	Ren Zi	11/30	Ren Wu	12/29	Xin Hai	1/28	Xin Si	26
27	9/3	Jia Yin	10/3	Jia Shen	11/1	Gui Chou	12/1	Gui Wei	12/30	Ren Zi	1/29	Ren Wu	27
28	9/4	Yi Mao	10/4	Yi You	11/2	Jia Yin	12/2	Jia Shen	12/31	Gui Chou	1/30	Gui Wei	28
29	9/5	Bing Chen	10/5	Bing Xu	11/3	Yi Mao	12/3	Yi You	1/1	Jia Yin	1/31	Jia Shen	29
30	9/6	Ding Si			11/4	Bing Chen			1/2	Yi Mao			30
	8 White		**7 Red**		**6 White**		**5 Yellow**		**4 Green**		**3 Jade**		
	Li Qiu 8/7 3:40pm		**Bai Lu** 9/7 7:01pm		**Han Lu** 10/8 11:04am		**Li Dong** 11/7 2:21pm		**Da Xue** 12/7 7:00am		**Xiao Han** 1/5 5:46pm		Jie
	Chu Shu 8/23 6:32am		**Qiu Fen** 9/23 4:37am		**Shuang Jiang** 10/23 2:15pm		**Xiao Xue** 11/22 11:46am		**Dong Zhi** 12/22 12:44am		**Da Han** 1/20 10:54am		Qi

The Principles of Feng Shui - Book One

After years of intensive research, experimentation, exploration and teaching of Feng Shui, Master Larry Sang put forth his accumulated knowledge and insights into this book. This book will systematically introduce Feng Shui to its readers. This book is recommended for our Beginning, Intermediate and Advanced Feng Shui classes.

Available in paperback and ebook. $18.75 US

Yi Jing for Love and Marriage

In the journey of life, we often experience times of doubt, confusion and feeling lost. What should we do when facing this type of situation? The Changing Hexagram Divination method can help by predicting what may happen. It can provide guidelines for coping with difficult situations or insight into beneficial ones. This book provides a simple method for the reader to predict the answers to their questions and to help others. Besides resolving confusion and doubt, it also provides a fun hobby for those interested in the ancient art of divination. Use this book as your consultant on Love and Marriage when the need arises!

Available in paperback and ebook. $14.75 US

Ten-Thousand Year Calendar (1882 - 2031)

Normally printed in Chinese, but now in English, this handy reference guide is what the Chinese call the Ten-Thousand Year Calendar. This calendar contains information for 150 years, from 1882 to 2031. It gives the annual, monthly, and daily stem and branch, the annual and monthly flying Star, as well as the lunar day of the month. It also gives information about the lunar and solar months, the solstices, equinoxes, and the beginning of the four seasons in the Chinese calendar. The Ten-Thousand Year Calendar is used for Feng Shui, Chinese Astrology, Day Selection, and various predictive techniques.

Available in ebook only. $26.00 US

Feng Shui Facts and Myths

This book is a collection of stories about Feng Shui and Astrology. Master Sang attempts to explain aspects of Feng Shui and Chinese Astrology, as the terms are understood or misunderstood in the West. This book will provide you with deeper information on the Chinese culture traditions of Feng Shui and Astrology.

Available in paperback and ebook. $16.00 US

Larry Sang's
2021 Chinese Astrology & Feng Shui Guide
The Year of The Ox

Each Section explains how to determine the key piece: determining your animal sign; how to read the Feng Shui of your home; and how to read the Day Selection calendar - a valuable day by day indication of favorable and unfavorable activity.

Available in paperback and ebook. $18.00 US

COURSE CATALOG

The following is a current list of the courses available from *The American Feng Shui Institute.* Please consult our online catalog for course fees, descriptions and new additions.

FENG SHUI

CLASS	CLASS NAME	PREREQUISITE
FS095	Introduction to Feng Shui	
FS101/OL	Beginning Feng Shui & Online	-
FS102/OL	Intermediate Feng Shui & Online	-
FS201/OL	Advanced Feng Shui & Online	FS101+FS102/OL
FS205/OL	Advanced Sitting and Facing & Online	FS101+FS102/OL
FS106/OL	Additional Concepts on Sitting & Facing	FS102/OL
FS225	Feng Shui Folk Beliefs	FS201
FS227/OL	Professional Skills for Feng Shui Consultants	FS201
FS231	Feng Shui Yourself & Your Business	FS201
FS235	Symptoms of a House	FS201
FS250	Explanation of Advanced Feng Shui Theories	FS201
FS275	9 Palace Grid and Pie Chart Graph Usage & Online	FS201
FS280	Advanced East West Theory	FS201
FS301	Advanced Feng Shui Case Study 1 & 2	FS201
FS303	Advanced Feng Shui Case Study 3 & 4 + Online	FS201
FS305/OL	Advanced Feng Shui Case Study 5 & Online	FS201
FS306/OL	Advanced Feng Shui Case Study 6 & Online	FS201
FS307/OL	Advanced Feng Shui Case Study 7 & Online	FS201
FS308/OL	Advanced Feng Shui Case Study 8 & Online	FS201
FS309	Advanced Feng Shui Case Study 9 & 10	FS201
FS311	Advanced Feng Shui Case Study 11	FS201
FS312/OL	Advanced Feng Shui Case Study 12	FS201
FS313/OL	Advanced Feng Shui Case Study 13 & Online	FS201 & AS101
FS314	Advanced Feng Shui Case Study 14	FS201
FS315	Advanced Feng Shui Case Study 15	FS201
FS316/FS317	Advanced Feng Shui Case Study 16 & 17	FS201
FS318/FS319	Advanced Feng Shui Case Study 18 & 19	FS201
FS320/FS321	Advanced Feng Shui Case Study 20 & 21	FS201
FS322/FS323	Advanced Feng Shui Case Study 22 & 23	FS201 & AS101
FS324/FS325	Advanced Feng Shui Case Study 24 & 25	FS201
FS326/FS327	Advanced Feng Shui Case Study 26 & 27	FS201

FENG SHUI - *continued from previous page*

FS340/OL	Secrets of the Five Ghosts	FS201
FS341	The Secrets of the "San Ban Gua"	FS201
FS260/OL	Lawsuit Support & Online	FS201 & AS101
FS270/OL	The Taisui, Year Breaker, Three Sha & Online	FS201 & AS101
FS350/OL	Feng Shui Day Selection 1 & Online	FS201 & AS101
FS351/OL	Feng Shui Day Selection 2 & Online	FS201 & FS350/OL
FS360/OL	Marriage and Life Partner Selection Online	FS201 & AS101
FS375/OL	Introduction to Yin House Feng Shui	FS201

YI JING

YJ101	Beginning Yi Jing Divination	AS101
YJ102	Yi Jing Coin Divination	AS101
YJ103	Plum Flower Yi Jing Calculation	AS101

CHINESE ASTROLOGY

AS101	Stems and Branches & Online	-
AS102	Four Pillars 1 & 2 (Zi Ping Ba Zi)	AS101 or AS101/OL
AS103	Four Pillars 3 & 4 (Zi Ping Ba Zi)	AS102
AS105	Four Pillars 5 & 6 (Zi Ping Ba Zi)	AS103
AS201A/OL	Beginning Zi Wei Dou Shu, Part 1	AS101
AS201B/OL	Beginning Zi Wei Dou Shu, Part 2	AS201A/OL
AS211/OL	Intermediate Zi Wei Dou Shu	AS201B/OL
AS301A/OL	Advanced Zi Wei Dou Shu, Part 1	AS211/OL
AS301B/OL	Advanced Zi Wei Dou Shu, Part 2	AS201A/OL
AS311/OL	Zi Wei Dou Shu Case Study 1 & Online	AS301B/OL
AS313/OL	Zi Wei Dou Shu Case Study 3 & Online	AS301B/OL
AS314	Zi Wei Dou Shu Case Study 2 & 4	AS301B/OL

CHINESE ARTS

CA101/OL	Palm & Face Reading 1 & 2	-
CA102	Palm & Face Reading 3 & 4	CA101 or CA101/OL
CA103	Palm & Face Reading for Health	-
CA121	Introduction to Chinese Medicine	-
CA110	Professional Face Reading	-

CHINESE PHILOSOPHY

CP101	Introduction to Daode Jing	-
CP102	Feng Shui Yourself	-

CLASSES AT THE
AMERICAN FENG SHUI INSTITUTE

Due to the limited seating capacity, reservations are necessary and seats are on a first come first serve basis. To reserve your seat, a $50.00 US deposit is required and is non-refundable if cancellation by student takes place less than three days before class. Please mail-in check or call us to reserve your seat with a credit card*. Balance is due on the first day of class.

Please DO NOT e-mail credit card information as this is not a secure method

ONLINE CLASSES WITH THE
AMERICAN FENG SHUI INSTITUTE FEATURE:

- Easy navigation
- Self tests at the end of each module
- A discussion board with trained Institute's Instructors
- Audio clips for pronunciation
- An online discussion board
- An instant feedback final exam

The online classes are self-paced study modules. They are segmented into four, one-week lessons that lead you at your own pace, over the four-week course. You have 60 days to complete the course work.

For more information, please see our website:
www.amfengshui.com

AMERICAN
FENG SHUI

INSTITUTE

7220 N. Rosemead Blvd.
Suite. 204
San Gabriel, CA 91775
Phone: (626) 571-2757

E-mail: fsinfo@amfengshui.com
amfengshui@gmail.com

AS A STUDENT OF
THE AMERICAN FENG SHUI INSTITUTE:

You will receive a certificate of completion from the American Feng Shui Institute, for the Beginning/Intermediate and Advanced Feng Shui Classes. Please do not confuse this certification as licensing, as there are no requirements for practitioner at this time.

As a student of the Institute, we are available to assist you with your studies. We have an online Bulletin Board for questions and answers, featuring a topic search. You will obtain access to the Bulletin Board upon completion of the Advance Feng Shui class. Due to the complexity of the courses, graduates may repeat in the classroom that you have already taken, pending available seats. Please see our online course catalog for the most current course offerings.

CANCELLATION AND REFUND POLICY:

All institutional charges shall be returned to the registrant less a $50.00 US cancellation fee, if cancellation notice is received prior to or on the first day of instruction. Any notification of withdrawal or cancellation and any request for a refund are required to be made in writing.

Refunds shall be made within thirty (30) days of receipt of the withdrawal or cancellation notice and refund request.

The institute does not participate in the Student Tuition Recovery Fund (STRF). We are registered with the State of California. Registration means we have met certain minimum standards imposed by the state for registered schools on the basis of our written application to the state. Registration does not mean we have met all of the more extensive standards required by the state for schools that are approved to operate or license or that the state has verified the information we submitted with our registration form.